6/24/98

On the Edge of the Wild

Passions and Pleasures of a Naturalist

Stephen Bodio

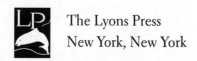
The Lyons Press
New York, New York

For LIBBY

Copyright © 1998 by Stephen J. Bodio

ALL RIGHTS RESERVED. No part of this book may be reproduced in any manner without the express written consent of the publisher, except in the case of brief excerpts in critical reviews and articles. All inquiries should be addressed to: The Lyons Press, 31 West 21 Street, New York, New York 10010.

Printed in the United States of America

10 9 8 7 6 5 4 3 2 1

Design by Joel Friedlander Publishing Services, San Rafael, CA

Library of Congress Cataloging-in-Publication Data

Bodio, Stephen.
    On the edge of the wild: passions and pleasures of a naturalist / Stephen Bodio.
    p. cm.
    Some essays were previously published in various journals.
    ISBN 1-55821-648-0
    1. Hunting—West (U.S.) 2. Natural history—West (U.S.) 3. Bodio, Stephen.
4. Country life—West (U.S.)
SK45.B64   1998
081—DC21   97-28147
                                                   CIP

Several essays in this book have been published before. Please see the end of each individual essay for the specific publication in which it first appeared.

"This, like his books, fuselage, imaginary garden, family, loves, religion, and private history was an indispensable component of the spiritual survival multiple he was inventing for himself, and through which he intended to sandwich himself between earth, sea, and stars with the fit a waffle has within a waffle iron, or the kind of mortising James Powell had performed in his skiff, less a seamlessness than the kind of laminated strength a scar has."

—Thomas McGuane, Ninety-Two in the Shade

Books by Stephen Bodio

A Rage for Falcons
Good Guns
The Art of Shooting Flying
Aloft
Querencia
Good Guns Again
On the Edge of the Wild

Contents

Apologia and Acknowledgments

This book is a collage in essays about the kind of life I have found worth living, so far.

It is a life lived far from the glossy images of popular culture; that much is obvious. Less obviously, it is also one that is uncomfortable with the increasingly product-oriented so-called sporting life portrayed in the high-quality magazines.

Although "green" readers will, I hope, find much to admire and think about in these pages, I do not share all their attitudes, either. "Look, don't touch" has never been an attitude I could take seriously. This life of mine believes in intimate contact, in eating and wallowing and breathing the dust, in sometimes getting the blood on its hands. See the epigraph. I don't think anyone can love anything without knowing it very well; I do *not* mean virtually, either.

Anyone who reads this book will find that common themes run through the essays. I have tried to see the words, at least, are not repetitive.

■

The acknowledgments here could be a problem; the temptation is to cite too few, or go on for pages. This book has been ten years in the making and owes a debt to people living and dead, ones I know and ones who don't know I exist. Here is a stab at a few.

First and foremost, my thanks to Libby, Elizabeth Adam Frishman Bodio, wife and partner, the best.

Second, to the other Elizabeth: Betsy Huntington, late best friend and partner, 1929–1986.

To several dogs, also gone: Bart, Sass, Maggie, Riley, and Luna.

To a bunch of friends in New Mexico: John Paul Jones Apachito, Constance Aylward, Frank Bond, John and Rebecca Daniel-Davila, Wade Dixon, Colleen Grayson, Phil Guerro and his family, Karl Hess Jr., Rudy Lucero, Floyd Mansell, Omar Qureshi and Christine Leister, M. H. Salmon, Tommy Torres and the late Shirley Tarpley, the former crew at Red Lake Ranch, the Pound family, and the staff of the Golden Spur Bar.

And in Montana and elsewhere: to Russ Chatham especially, for everything; to John Baden, John Barsness and Eileen Clarke, Chuck Bowden, Ralph Buscemi, Kent Carnie, Marc and Linda Clarke, Bernard Cole of William Evans, Ltd., Tim Crawford, Mark Fanning, John Graves, Linda Hasselstrom, Jane Jarrett; to Tom McGuane for quotes and more; to Peter Martin, Rosalyn and Robert Mayberry, Dan McCarron, Pere Henri Michel, M. R. Montgomery, Dan O'Brien, Doug Peacock, Datus Proper, Annie Proulx, David Quammen and Kris Ellingsen, Tom and Jeri Quinn, George Reiger, Charles Schwartz, Pierre Stoyanovich, Tom Torres Jr., both Fred Turners, Jim Weaver, and Eric Wilcox.

To my agent and friend, Cassandra Leoncini.

To a few editors: Nick Lyons, and Ed and Becky Gray, first and foremost; John Thorne, and Mark Zanger; to Don Snow and Deb Clow; to Jim Butler, Steve Smith, Chuck Johnson, and, more recently, Allen Jones.

And to a couple of writers who don't know I exist, whose thoughts inform this particular book: to Sven Birkerts and Ferenc Maté. This is my odd attempt at "A Reasonable Life."

—*Stephen Bodio*
Magdalena, New Mexico

PART I

The Country

Struck with
Consequence

A Canadian journalist wrote a few years ago that people like me—
"male writers and artists"—live in the West mainly because
things stay the same, because what you loved one day you could be
forgiven for loving the next. I don't think the motive is ignoble, or
restricted to males. I have lived for sixteen years now in a determinedly
unchic western town whose charms are obscure, austere, sometimes
even squalid, and so far I have been forgiven for all that I love. But I
like another of that journalist's quotes better: "The wilderness reminded him that everything he did had a consequence."

We fell in love with the country first. For coastal people, the Real
West is wilder and more full of marvels than they can imagine without living in it . . . or, often, even when they do begin to live in it. The
heart of the West will always be the big dry blue blocks of forest service and BLM land, cut into spaces the size of New England states by
highways and New West boomtowns. Off in their centers, invisible to
travelers, are whole worlds. But there is so much going on at the edges
that it takes a while to get to them. In my first months in New Mexico I saw a bobcat in my yard and picked up an unfortunate adolescent

lion's skull in the arroyo that flowed through town. I flushed golden eagles from the highway's edge, and climbed to falcon aeries that overlooked pavement. Ravens—in my other life rare denizens of the coast of Maine—were now rarely out of sight. Rattlesnakes were a common summer nuisance; every other week or so, I'd move a prairie rattler from my yard and release it behind the town dump. Antelope and scaled quail came to my fence by day, deer and elk crossed the road by night. I had never lived in a place so full of wild creatures—not just managed species like deer and elk but raptors, songbirds, an ark of reptiles, javelinas, coyotes, three species of foxes, lions, bears, and rumors of wolves.

That we hunted, just like everybody else, was at first a source of amazement to our neighbors, then a road into the country and new friendships. My partner, who took all things as she found them, had the easier way; that she could ride well didn't hurt, either. I was solitary and set in my ways, a falconer and bird hunter and naturalist who had a social and aesthetic dislike of such things as deer drives: in short, a bit of a snob, though I didn't realize it. She had no such problems. Once she got a job on the local paper, reporting on rodeos and fairs and traveling seventy miles to town meetings, there was no holding her back. It wasn't until after her death that I realized how friendships with western country people transcend even death. Her friends had now become mine.

We had known a few ranchers together while she was alive. John, a young landowner who lived where he was born, thirty miles south of the pavement, showed up after a cryptic preliminary call with a goshawk on his fist. It was not an imprinted modern falconer's servant with enough paper on it to license a liquor store, but a wild old bird that had gone through about twenty fifty-dollar fighting-cock chicks before John live-trapped it with a set of monofilament snares and decided to ask the advice of the only falconer in the county, seventy-five miles away. I don't know who looked more feral that day—John, a pale caballero slumped in my chair wearing denim and snakeskin boots and a black tractor cap, with a raptorial nose and an Okie-sounding twang at odds with his land-grant surname; or the hawk. The gos was an old breeder, a "haggard" in falconers' terminology, with eyes that had darkened with age past ruby to garnet. Although he wasn't much bigger than a pigeon, he was as spooky up close as an uncaged leopard and as elegant as an ancient engraving of death. Except for his eyes and legs he was a study in monochrome, with the black back of the Sierra Madre "Apache" race, and eyebrows and front of filigreed silver. He gripped John's work-gloved fist with spidery yellow fingers and watched our every move, but made no attempt to fly.

I was impressed by their cool. "Looks like you've already got him manned."

"I ain't done much. He's not stupid."

"What do you expect to do with him?"

"I don't know. Put him back and let him make more, I guess. Seems a shame to keep him. . . ."

"What about your chickens?"

"He's worth fifty damn chickens."

I was amused and a little shocked. "Then why'd you catch him?"

"He was so neat, I just sort of wanted to see him up close."

A lot of the older ranchers would not have agreed; they were fond of poisons, and shot every rattlesnake. But after Betsy died I began to meet back-country people who shared John's sentiments. Sis, a matriarch-in-training, heiress apparent to a four-generation ranch established by an Italian Swiss in the 1880s, a team roper, bartender, and community activist, wouldn't kill a snake, though she always carried a .38. She collected them live for the university, and once sketched for me the crucial difference in labial scale count between the Mojave and western diamondback rattlers on a bar napkin. Her brothers, who ran a guide service and a lion pack but who disliked the sometimes necessary killing of lions, had snapped Polaroids of virtually every local lion, each perched defiantly on a tree or ledge, and could tell them apart by their tracks. Still later I met Windy Will, a slightly older small rancher in the badlands to the north, who read Edward Abbey, grinning and shaking his head ("I approve of the sorry-ass son-of-a-bitch at least half the time") and who argued against making a local peak a designated wilderness only because it would then fill up with people from Albuquerque.

Something that should have been obvious dawned on me slowly. First and foremost, contrary to those who portray ranchers as profit-hungry, greedy exploiters, interested only in squeezing the most out of the land, monsters who somehow manage to combine the worst characteristics of capitalist consumption and welfare abuse: *The ranchers love their land.*

All their land, deeded and leased. They, at least those who live on it—that most ranchers are absentee landlords is slander—know every inch of it as well as you know your backyard. (And if you care enough to read these words, I suspect you know your backyard better than 80 percent of the populace.) They've ridden over it, lived and died on it. They have stories, song lines: Here's where Uncle Pancho was shot by those sons-of-bitches in 1918; here's where the bobcats den; hawk nests up there; here's where Billy damn near cut his hand off with the chain saw in '75. Some of them are even good stewards. In time, they have been changed from Europeans with a fear of all that is wild to people who have quirky affection for all those strange things out there: the singing coyotes, dark ominous eagles, invisible mountain lions—all these fellow inhabitants that you have to put up with but that finally make your home a very different place than the suburbs of New York City.

They also love work, hard work, on that same land. Though not routines. I've rarely met happier people than cowboys who have work. Nor ones who hate "regular hours" more, which may point to one of the reasons ranch folks are hard for outsiders to understand. Urban-

6

ites, yuppies, suburbanites, call them what you will: They are all middle class, bourgeois, with jobs and routines from which they escape to an increasingly intricate web of pleasures. Ranchers and cowboys, whether owners or workers, stand outside this twentieth-century structure. They control baronial amounts of land, but their customs and language seem working class to intellectuals. They have the frugality and generosity, the sir-and-ma'am manners of the plain people of the South, from whom their culture descends. They are emotional, contrary to the John Wayne image, and can be moved to tears. But they don't show their tears to strangers.

A Montana friend pointed toward a real difference between "modern" and country people. She said that urbanites tend to see all people who work with the soil and nature—farmers and fishermen as well as ranchers and cowboys—as people who are losers in the professional race, "people too dumb to be yuppies," people too unintellectual to have real jobs. Because of this, they can be pitied but hardly consulted on important issues. And those who are out there in the employer class must be in it to make money off the land, to rape it as long as they are allowed—why else would anyone live voluntarily in W. H. Auden's "desert full of bigots"?

There is consequence here, all around.

I came to romanticize ranchers a bit, which didn't much interest them one way or the other. Defending them against a compulsory multiculturalism in which European whites were the new inferior class, I forgot the true lesson of multiculturalism: that we're all equal, equally fucked, European and Indian and African and Mexican, that even a dog is capable of cruelty, that some sort of original sin exists, that Buddhism demands compassion for a reason. I dreamed of a place where the best of the Old and the New West would come together, where long-haired cowboys and literate tough cowgirls and sensitive hunters would stand together against the exploiters and Californicators, the miners and vegetarians. The wave crested when a ranch cou-

7

ple my own age and I vowed to secede from the larger county and form our own, with guns blazing for ranchers and hunters, readers and rattlesnakes. I started a book on the strength of such euphoria, intending an explanation of ranchers to the coast, a manifesto for environmentally sound ranching, I don't know what else. It collapsed. Feelings were hurt, money was lost. People for the West, that cynically funded exploiter of legitimate paranoia, claimed my friends. "Environmentalist" became a swear word, and spotted owls a joke. I wrote a novel, but never sold it.

My town still looks the same. There is no skiing here, and no blue-ribbon trout water; we're a hundred miles from the nearest city with jobs. And yet: In the last year we've elected a mayor who has lived here three years. Two galleries have opened, both selling "southwestern art." There is talk of a leash law, and trash fees; the dump is now routinely referred to as the sanitary landfill, and has hours. You can no longer leave dead animals there. Of course, People for the West is stronger than ever; the bumper sticker of choice is BOBBIT BABBITT.

■

The rumor goes like this: A lion "stalked" a kid from a new family upcanyon. There's a consensus: Everybody wants to kill it, but the Christians and the new people are most fervent. The new people *say* they're reluctant. In the old days the cat might have been killed, but not talked to death by hypocrites. Of course, the lion probably doesn't care much about the various rationales.

I contemplate moving: Provence, Chihuahua, Thailand. I hear John's in Belize.

■

The old people, the old cultures, knew something about consequence that the new ones don't. The new ones, both born again and politically correct (two faces of the same coin, or hydra, eerily similar in their self-righteousness), are of course sure they know, surer than

8

the old ones ever are. Luigi Barzini, the Italian journalist, once wrote of such people that "they lack the humble skills of men who have to work with lackadaisical unpredictable nature, the skills so to speak of sailors, fishermen, farmers, horsetamers, the people who must at all costs avoid deceiving themselves and must develop prudence, patience, skepticism, resignation, as well as great fortitude and perseverance."

What the old ones really knew in their bones was that death exists, that all life eats and kills to eat, that all lives end, that energy goes on. They knew that humans are participants, not spectators. Their work and play and rituals affirmed and reinforced this knowledge.

The new ones all want to evade death and deny it, legislate against it, transcend it. They run, bicycle, network, and pray. They stare into their screens and buy their vitamins. Here, they want the street drunks locked up, cigarettes banned, drunken driving met with more severe penalties than armed assault. They fear guns, cowboys, Muslims, pit bulls, whiskey, homosexuals, and freedom. Strong smells offend them.

In my town, the new people are disgusted by the *matanzas* of the old Spanish culture. Who but the Spanish and Mexicans would call a joyous fiesta celebrating pork a *matanza*, a "killing"?

The new ones hate dangerous hard work. Who but a cretin would voluntarily work on horseback, rope cows, unroll miles of barbed wire? Or, for that matter, cut trees, stack bricks, fish out of sight of shore in winter, plow, balance on high steel? They fear solitude and people who don't babble. When they are alone or silent, thoughts of death or meaninglessness come flooding in. Who would be alone? For this reason, they fear real leisure, and distrust anyone, rich or poor, who has too much.

They like games but don't know how to play. They dislike the idea of skills—that anyone might do anything better than anyone else. They distract themselves with endless interchangeable electronic fantasies, none too different or disturbing. Real novels deal with hard things—a woman I once dated told me they were all about dysfunctional families—and must be assimilated in solitude, so nobody reads. They raise their children with Nintendo.

New people say the word *spiritual* a lot. They have never looked long into any void. They prefer the Paradise Valley to the Red Desert. They pray for angels, extraterrestrials, the rapture, rescue, intervention. They believe in recovered memories, but have few real ones. They think they are victims, but they are conquerors.

According to an article in *High Country News*, "an important regional representative" from a national conservation organization said in a meeting in Aspen that "the role of environmental groups is to save the Colorado Plateau from the people who live there."

The new people disapprove of, cannot comprehend, hunting. How could anybody but a sadist cause death voluntarily, again and again? That they also do so escapes their tender consciences and consequence-free brains. Curiously, they allow and even celebrate catch-and-release fly fishing. Some of its practitioners are even what conservation writer Ted Kerasote calls "fossil fuel vegetarians." I know a woman who persecuted—not too strong a verb—a fellow worker because he had drawn a sheep permit and backpacked into a remote wilderness peak, then out of it with the head and the meat. She is so devoted to nouveau fishing that she had a beaver dam on her property dynamited. As Dave Barry says, "I am not making this up."

The "instinct to hunt," whatever that is, must be strong, else why would a bunch of death deniers spend the budget of a medium-size Third World country on chic equipment for what a colder mind might call "fish torture"? They think they are innocent, and brag that they do not eat fish. They leave their fingerprints on the river, their footprints on the gravel; many leave uneaten fish floating downstream. The greener among them are merely self-righteous and maybe—to use a phrase I usually don't—in denial. The more egregious offenders in the same army squeeze whitefish, bash carp, fight returning river habitats to native coarse fish because they prefer brown trout.

I have fly fished since I was four; still do. I tell people that "pure" catch-and-release is playing without consequence, date rape, politically correct torture for the sentimental. I get some odd looks.

Gary Synder says: "Life in the wild is not just eating berries in the sunlight. I like to imagine a 'depth ecology' that would go to the dark side of nature . . . the ball of crunched bones in the scat, the feather in the snow, the tales of insatiable appetite." Too abstract? He continues: "The other side of the 'sacred' is the sight of your beloved in the underworld, dripping with maggots." Can you live with the thought of that consequence?

Buddhist hermits, nurses, and cowboys see death as real, horrible, inevitable, necessary, unimportant, and sometimes funny. One night when my partner Betsy was still alive, we got to drinking hard with John and his wife. I believe it was after a cockfight fiesta, and a meal of Burmese-style curry, with cinnamon and chilies and black Chinese mushrooms. Gradually conversation turned to what we later referred to as "dead-animal stories" . . . absurd deaths, horrible ones, hilarious ones. From there, inevitably, it progressed to human death tales. There was a chill outside the ring around the woodstove, and fire in our bellies. I doubt four people ever laughed harder. There were tears in all our eyes and my sides hurt. I could barely sit in a chair.

The evening after Betsy died, John and Becky materialized outside the Albuquerque house where I was staying, a square bottle of brown whiskey in John's hand. Betsy's older sister, China born, silver haired, impeccably Episcopal, was staying there as well. We sat around all evening, passing the bottle — not "killing" it but transforming its substance to story, using it to retrieve memories, to offer them with more than our usual eloquence. We told Betsy stories, and one of them was the night of dead-animal stories. Then we told dead-animal stories. We all of us, including Jane, laughed so hard and so inappropriately that we horrified our proper hosts. Telling stories of life and death that made us laugh and weep was exactly the right way to mourn. But for the fact that there was a gaping ragged-edged hole in my life, it might have been one of the best evenings I had ever spent.

■

Eagles. Right now I'm writing a book about golden eagles. How can somebody proper, somebody hedged by written rules, somebody who has never taken his or her food from the ground or brought it down from the air, have a chance to understand an eagle? They are so *other*—almost as old as dinosaurs, with eyes bigger than their brains, which yet contain an intelligence as eager as a dog's. They weigh ten pounds and can inflict thousands of pounds of pressure at their talon points. They kill their siblings, then stay absolutely loyal to their mates for thirty years. They can pick a grouse out of the air at two hundred miles per hour or, in a harsh winter, tear at an antelope's side until it totters in circles and falls dead. What could they think of us? That we eat dirt and stones and things that do not move, crawl in motion on the face of the earth, and kill at a distance? How can sentimentalists make them little people in bird suits, or moralists make them evil?

(On the other hand: I was cutting wood with a friend, an old Comanche from Oklahoma, a couple of years ago, when a coyote came down a hill and barked at us. I went up to put a little sensible fear into him—not all humans find his kind as amusing as Leonard and I do. He came closer and barked again. Fianlly, I pulled off my hat and ran straight at him, whooping. He trotted off, looking over his shoulder. When I returned, Leonard was muttering something about goddamn stupid Eyetalian Yankees.

"What, Leonard?"

"Forget it."

"I'm serious. What's the matter?"

He finally permitted himself a smile. "Well, anyway, he was talkin' to you. I don't know why I was worried . . . it's all on your head."

"What?"

"Either money or death. We'll know when we get back to town. Shut up and load."

As a matter of fact, it was money—a book advance, as we found out when we got to the bar. I should add that I don't believe this story. What's money to a coyote?)

■

So, again, what? I am one without solutions. We're all screwed, remember? We all await death where we are, playing or not, seeing or not, accepting consequence or denying it. It is easier to be awake, easier not to be a somnambulist, in some places than others. The phrase *last best places* scares the piss out of me. Use it and lose it—besides, what does "last" mean? Still, I had hoped we might grow a different kind of culture here.

Doing what, exactly? Maybe living with and in, not "off" or beside, the land and its creatures. Christians kill predators. The echt-Greenie thinks he or she kills nothing, and is deluded. Better to eat and respect. Consequence. Those who avoid or deny those choices think evolution, or God, got it wrong. I don't.

"And as for small difficulties and worryings, prospects of sudden disaster, peril of life and limb; all these, and death itself, seem to him only sly good-natured hints, and jolly punches in the side bestowed by some unseen and unaccountable old joker." A hermit monk in the foothills of the Tien Shan? No, Herman Melville.

Eat and respect. Cultivate your garden, on your hands and knees. Eat weird things like lion and hawk; taste the wild; save roadkills. Eat a cow from a good rancher; know who the good ranchers are. Eat deer constantly. Hunt mushrooms.

If you are female, hunt. If you are male, hunt with, and converse with, those outside the fraternity. Dogs are a start. But how about your wife, children, falcon, horse, ferret, neighbor? Befriend your weapons and tools, and the people next door.

The West we inhabit, the Next West we will, should not be a suburb or a text or a landscape photograph, all glossy and flat, but the Real West, an intricate mosaic in motion whose uncountable facets are rocks, birds, mammals, rivers, people, ourselves. It has a meaning apart from us, which we can only partly comprehend. Its history is full of heroism, pain, and horror, like all history; its future is unknowable. We can save the parts, but we can't freeze-dry it or edit it. Living in it beats watching it. Releasing a trout still leaves a mark on the river.

The Real West is something wild and edged; like life, it makes us sad just at the moment we think we've caught it, the moment at which we are most struck with its beauty and consequence. Sooner or later we must leave it all, and the knowledge breaks our hearts. We can live with this knowledge, and celebrate it; it keeps us honest. But if we treat the country as a television set or a backdrop, if we fail to see it and its myriad inhabitants, from deer mouse to rancher, as real, then it will first bore us and then leave us behind—even as we slap down another payment on the lease. Haven't we done this enough times already?

—*Northern Lights* (1995)

Moving to Montana

My first sight of Montana was through the window of a Greyhound bus.

It was 1971. I was, incredibly, divorced, though barely old enough to vote. I was headed on impulse to Washington State, to hang out with an old friend in the biology department at Pullman. There were practical aspects to that visit that have no place here, but I had another agenda, hidden even to myself except at the edge of sleep. Montana, even then, looked to be a place where I could invent myself out of a handful of contradictory fascinations I could not resolve in Massachusetts.

For instance, I was in many ways a conventional rebel of those times: hair past my shoulders, a taste for illegal substances and rock and roll, and a devotion to Jack Kerouac, Ken Kesey, and Richard Brautigan.

But I also loved fishing and hunting with an unholy passion, despite the disapproval of my friends in Cambridge and Boston. I loved all of it, all the time, and with a fire that burned hotter than it ever can again. In the summer, I crawled up streams under thick alder tangles just to hold, for a moment, five-inch native brook trout with colors better than any trout ever painted. I froze on winter sandbars within earshot of the surf for a chance at scoters, shooting an Iver John-son so worn that it doubled about every third shot; I haunted ceme-teries and golf courses for rabbits and gray squirrels with my faithful redtail; I cast immense, awkward eelskin rigs from eleven-foot, revolv-ing-spool surf-casting rods into the Cape Cod Canal, trying for the last of the big cow stripers.

Deer hunting meant taking a stand in the cedar swamps where visibility might be only fifty feet. Rifles weren't allowed; my deer gun was a humpbacked Browning autoloader I still own, a "sweet-six-teen" loaded with slugs ahead of buckshot. I used the same gun for grouse in even denser cover; it was choked too tight, but it was what I had. I remember the astonishment in the eyes of two proper Yan-kees who toted a Parker and what I now think was a Purdey when I emerged from their covert in blue jeans and a denim shirt, my long hair held back with a blue and white bandanna, and that evil gun over my arm. They were polite, but I suspect I embodied their nightmares.

I had other dreams. Ernest Thompson Seton had fed my child-hood on Lobo and the Pacing Mustang and various western dogs, on the tale of the jackrabbit he called the Little Warrior. Even as I wept over the fate of his heroes (most Seton protagonists die miserable deaths), I was also devouring hunting stories by Russell Annabel and Elmer Keith, Ernest Hemingway and Jack O'Connor. I knew there were other ways to do things. There were trout out there more than sixteen inches long, in rivers where you could cast without hitting a tree with your rod. Deer and antelope stood belly deep in sage (what-ever that was); you had to be careful not to silhouette yourself on the skyline. You shot a .270, of course, a pre-'64 Winchester Model 70 with a classic stock.

There were more contemporary temptations as well. Western fal-coners were alleged to be training Arctic gyrfalcons to attack mighty sage grouse on the plains of Wyoming and Montana. There were stories about Jim Weaver, a falconry legend even before he ran the peregrine recovery project at Cornell, walking into the Charles M. Russell with a gyrfalcon on his fist, a daypack, a bedroll, matches, and a German shorthair, to appear a week later as well fed and rested as an active falconer could be.

And, the grapevine had it, there were strange activities near Livingston. A bunch of young sportsmen as crazy as I were camped there, writing and drinking and talking and helling around, fishing and shooting birds and dreaming big dreams. It seemed there might be a place for me in the West, where you could be young and wild but also a gentleman of literature, where you could appreciate a Parker and an Adams, a 7x57 and a Leonard rod, not to mention both Turgenev and Edward Abbey.

I didn't find any of this on my first trip; I was too distracted to make new friends in any case. My moods ran more to solitary drinking and chain-smoking unfiltered Camels. What I found was something more important: the sheer physical and sensory impact of the West. Out first stop, somewhere east of Miles City, was before dawn. As a shaft of light pierced a black horizon bigger than the ocean, I felt my lungs expand for what felt like the first time in months, then relax. Tears sprang to my eyes. I felt that the world was bigger than I'd ever realized back in New England. I turned to see a juniper and a white-faced steer glowing in the impossibly clear air. A magpie leaped from the tree and started the world again, trailing its shining ribbon of tail, and I knew with absolute certainty I'd be back.

Other epiphanies were to come. My first sight of real mountains (forget forever New England's hills), lit at the top like icebergs with a light that I had never seen before but that I would remember with a sort of Proustian flood of senses twenty-five years later in front of a little Bierstadt in the Nygard Gallery in Bozeman. A brilliant cinnamon teal drake curving to drop into a pond near Butte. A herd of white-tailed deer feeding out into a meadow west of Billings at dusk. (I doubt

I ever saw one that far from a tree in Massachusetts.) They all confirmed my first decision, which became "West," but not Montana.

Ten years after my first sight and decision found me in the Gila-Mogollon country of New Mexico, one of my childhood realms of escape, writing for a living. Some of those Livingstonites became long-distance friends in the way writers do, mostly by mail, as did some of those falconers. All of us were writing about the West and sport and other passions, living lives we had fantasized when we were kids reading magazines and books that formed us more than our parents did.

And then my partner Betsy died. My life turned to chaos. After a year of roaming and drinking and attempting to bring some kind of order to my existence, I wrote the story of our New Mexico home, our birds and dogs and hunting, our life, her death. The publisher who had commissioned it backed out, and I feared I was going down the drain. In a last desperate act I asked Jamie Harrison, then working for Russell Chatham's brand-new Clark City Press, if she might show the manuscript to her father, Jim Harrison, who might tell me if it was worth a damn. I thought Clark City was to be a fine-art press for Russ, and was shocked when she called back a week later with a generous offer that included the painting now gracing the cover of that book, *Querencia.*

Montana, and Montana sport, became a door back into sanity for the second time. Russ Chatham lent me a Suburban when I flew up, a suite at the Murray, a shotgun, sometimes the whole house at Deep Creek. There were ruffed grouse in the willows in little drainages that led up into the Absarokas, blue grouse in the willows in little drainages that led up north toward the Crazies, brook trout as brilliant as the ones of my youth (but three times bigger) in a little pond somewhere up above Chico.

Russ introduced me to a woman he knew, a widow, a professional cook and mail-order executive, who could drop a cast of wet flies exactly where she wanted, who knew where the wild ("not yuppie") trout were. For my part, I taught her about bird hunting and falconry, and bought her a lady's gun from another Montana writer. I began to commute—if driving every few months between houses twelve hundred miles apart can be called commuting. I vacillated between 28-bore quail guns and big 12s for sage birds, settling on a little English side-by-side 16. We learned how to be together in both places.

This month, September, Libby Frishman and I are marrying, in the little Episcopal church in Bozeman, marrying each other and joining our two communities. In a sense we're marrying two states, two states of mind, two sets of friends, two still-magnificent ecosystems. The separate pulls and sports of New Mexico and Montana might be the subject of another column, but that's for later. Right now, we're headed south. We'll be back in November. Montana, if not just Montana, feels like home.

—*Big Sky Journal* (1996)

from Tiger Country

> *. . . When I got back I showed the pictures to my karate instructor. He's a mean old Korean, about sixty-five, head like a bowling ball . . . anyway he looked at the mountains and said, "Are tigers here?"*
>
> *"No sir," I said. "We got deer and elk and black bear and mountain lion. Used to have wolves, and jaguar, and bigger bears. No tigers."*
>
> *He looked at me like I was a little slow. "Looks like tiger country to me."*
>
> *—Excerpt from a letter*

Think of a dry plateau the size of Connecticut . . . maybe a little bigger, with an average height above sea level of, oh, seven thousand feet. That's right—the flat ground is "higher" than Vermont's mountains. Brown plains, nappy and dry like a lion-colored pool table.

Add the following: not just a few but many mountain chains, most north–south; one going more east–west; all reaching above nine and, some, ten thousand feet; blue with pine and fir and spruce. No ponds or lakes, natural ones anyway, but lots of snow in the winter, especially above eight thousand feet. Vertical weather. A day–night temperature difference of forty degrees, winter and summer.

People never made much impact here. The paved roads run around the edges; only one goes "through," so to speak, and it's two cars wide and twisty as a snake. There are two thousand people on the plateau today, more or less, most of them in towns where the only pavement is the road through.

The size of western land, and the distance you can see across it, baffles by its apparent openness. East of the Mississippi you can drive almost anywhere on paved roads, and find signs of human occupation wherever you go. You bring these assumptions West as surely as the first European settlers brought theirs. One of the hardest preconceptions to throw off is that, because you've seen the West from the interstate, you've seen the West. That forty-mile stretch between exits may be forty miles without a single paved crossing, or the interstate exit itself may give out to a dirt ranch road. You may drive a hundred miles at right angles to that exit before you hit a paved crossing. What you've just defined by its edges is a block bigger than Rhode Island or Delaware, with no pavement in it.

The interior of this block is likely to be rugged, impassable, and, except in Texas, owned by the federal government, aka you and me. Anyplace where there are real mountains is likely to include national forest; places without forest will be owned by the Bureau of Land Management; around the edges of these blocks, or mixing inextricably with them, are the ranches. There are more than a few big ranches—big because it's so dry. In most of the West ranchers own bottomlands and springs. But in order to have enough year-round pasture to make a living, they lease vast tracts of BLM and forest service land. Nobody here is getting rich.

This part of New Mexico is still the real West. It's a long way from Santa Fe and Taos, from tourists and New Age entrepreneurs and crystal miracles, from silver 'n' turquoise everything and coyotes with bandannas and neo–Native American art. It's a long dry drive to the near-est ski slope, Mercedes Benz, or Arab horse.

It's a long way from most regular western history, too. It's a five-hour drive over mountains to the high plains and all their romantic ghosts—Comanche, buffalo, lobo wolf. It's the same distance to Four Corners and the Navajo nation. It's a fair drive even to White Sands and its interesting legacy of stolen ranches, Oppenheimer, and the Bomb. It's a whole nation away from the Spanish land-grant north, that strange mix of Europe and America, with its sheep and Penitentes and trout streams and little churches with peaked tin roofs.

Most of its history is prehistory: the Pleistocene. The Old Ones, the Anasazi (a Navajo name—we don't know what they called themselves), were here for a good part of their cryptic history, and left one famous ruin and hundreds of smaller ones, many still undis-turbed.

The Apaches followed. For a while they were invincible in these, their woods and mountains. The horse soldiers under General Crook finally beat them with superior numbers and strategy; the soldiers held the water holes and harassed the Indians down into Mexico. Crook never beat them on tactics, though.

The miners flourished after the Apaches. They made a lot of holes and took away various things that were useful to them. But except for the open copper pit at Santa Rita, way down south, and a bunch of what look like caves, the miners' traces are fading faster than the Anasazi's.

Finally, there were the ranchers. They were good, tough men and women, and we should not dignify the craven attacks on them that are part of the historical moment's required attitudes. But all of the "Old" Spanish and New Anglo alike were of European descent, and they did exactly what their ancestors had done: They fought what they thought was a necessary war against their competitors, animal and human.

A few held on. Black bears, some black and shiny, others the color of Irish setters, adapt pretty well to humans, especially by *their* standards. They raid beehives and garbage cans and climb telephone poles when they get confused. They are wonderful animals, but they often act more like pretty pigs or giant raccoons than Real Bears. The Plains tribes knew the difference.

And there are cougars, still. (You should prefer that name to *lion*. It's American; besides, there's nothing lionlike about them.) Deer are their fodder, and we still have plenty of deer. Besides, the cougars are invisible.

And, of course, coyotes are everywhere. They are smart and sophisticated, have a sense of humor, and know what to fear. They are so little threat to cattle that cowmen, as opposed to sheepmen — "wool-growers" they call them now — treat coyotes with a mixture of affection and contempt, at least when they don't feel a need to test their rifles. Besides, coyotes can live on juniper berries and mice when the going gets tough.

But the real competitors are gone, or changed beyond recognition. The Apaches have achieved at least one small victory: On their reservations they now charge rich white men and Japanese industrialists the price of a small car to shoot carefully nurtured and prespotted bull elk, a ritual that these clients honestly think is hunting rather than a sort of decadent agriculture.

The Real Bears — Plains Indian for grizzly — and the real wolves, and the "tigers" — what the Mexicans call the jaguars — are just gone. Europeans never did get along with wolves and brown bears, for good reason. In our own Dream Time, bears competed with us for housing and meat, and wolves lived lives so much like ours that we made up stories of their exchanging shapes with us. When we began living in one place and keeping prey as our property, the war began in earnest. We brought it across the ocean with us, north across the Big River, west across the Plains. Wolves ran hit-and-run guerrilla strikes against us, just like the Apaches did. Contemporary accounts, trying hard to insult both tribes, are full of comparisons.

The bears—though they didn't constantly run off young stock the way the wolves did—were even more frightening. A grizzly could, and would, kill a human. In the fall, when the coming winter sharpened their appetites, they'd raid down out of their mountain fortresses like goblin kings, like Grendel. A big one could carry off a full-grown long-horn steer if that was his notion. If you chased him with hounds, he'd run till you couldn't hear the dogs, then turn and kill them all. If you caught up with him on horseback, he might charge faster than the horse could run. If you dismounted to shoot, there was no guarantee that a puny nineteenth-century black powder load would so much as slow the bear down before he mashed you to a pulp.

The pioneer stockmen were not people who expected, asked, or gave quarter. They hunted down every grizzly and wolf they could find, though "hunted" has a sporting connotation that I doubt many of these warriors ever felt. Government agents like Ben Lilly made their cause a religious crusade against servants of the Devil; Lilly considered defenders of predators to be heretics. Empathy is a grace rarely granted to foot soldiers.

One government agent had a change of heart. Aldo Leopold himself, patron saint of the modern conservation movement, was once a hired gun, an ace predator controller. But right here in the heart of his country he saw certain things in a dying wolf's eyes, and it changed him. When they killed the last grizzly on Escudilla he dared to speak the heretical truth: that it was only a mountain now.

The last Real Bear in the southwestern United States held on for a few more years; his skin came out of the high Magdalenas on the plateau's eastern edge in 1930, on the back of a burro. The last jaguar in New Mexico died in the snows of the Continental Divide here in 1903, victim of an alarmed ranch wife with a bucket of poisoned milk. The wolves, with their social intelligence, hung on longer. Their bands retreated across the Rio Grande into Old Mexico, as the Apaches did before them. The government mopped up the survivors with traps and poison in a campaign that lasted until the sixties. And don't think such methods weren't used against wild humans, in crueler or at least less sentimental times; or aren't elsewhere, today.

The country still does look real, though.

CutBank (1993)

An Unexpected Eagle

It was my second morning in France, and I was still disoriented and jet lagged, but I knew I had to go out. Behind the village rose a hill that revealed itself to be the first in a range, covered with oaks the height of the piñon amd juniper back home in New Mexico. Miles to the east, I could see the blue triangle of Mont Ventoux on the horizon.

She came out of the corner of my eye, beating upward and uphill, against the mistral. My instant impression, almost as instantly corrected, was that she resembled a harrier or marsh hawk . . . something about her long crooked wings. But I realized immediately that she was huge, five feet or more across her sails. She was cruising at tree level, checking the ground carefully, pausing between the crowns of the little oaks. As she drew close, she turned her head to study me.

I had never seen anything quite like her. Her head was big, round, and owlish; her eyes yellow and brilliant in the hazy spring sun. Her back and head were brown, her underparts dazzling white. The American bird she resembled most, at least superficially, was an osprey. But no osprey would be working over this dry hillside of *garrigue*, mixed oak and pine and scrub.

She seemed unalarmed. She hovered like a monstrous kestrel, her head swiveling to keep me in view, her legs dangling; then she changed her course and angled across the hillside toward Serignan in one powerful, effortless curve.

I realized that I knew, at least in theory, what she was—not because I expected to see her, for I, like most western North Americans, had thought of Europe as some kind of a garden *cum* museum, but because of my lifelong fascination with birds of prey. She was a short-toed or serpent eagle, the only European representative of a varied Old World family of raptors that specialize in snakes. She was not only a birder's life-list check but also a new family, a whole new kind of bird. I was ecstatic; seeing something so large and wild had instantly transformed my trip, a pilgrimage to one of the pioneer entomologists, Jean-Henri Fabre, into something a little more expeditionary, less purely scholarly. Back "home" in Serignan I confirmed her identity, checking in my French language guide to learn her more colorful Gallic name: *circaete de Jean-le-Blanc.*

Several days later I had already fallen into the new habit of taking dawn walks in the Bois de la Ranjarde. That morning I hadn't even reached the hilltop when I came upon two men dressed in camouflage loading two dogs into the back of a Deux Chevaux "truck." (I don't know exactly what to call these ubiquitous French rural vehicles; they resemble a little pickup truck with a built-in box behind the cab.) The men were as different as their canine companions. The larger was baby faced and mustached, with a cap, and held a huge shaggy white hound on a chain. His smaller companion, sharp featured, wiry, and dark with an unfiltered cigarette clenched in his mouth, looked like the archetypal blue-collar Provençal and could have been a relative of mine. His dog was to all appearances a sweet little black-and-tan coon hound.

They gave me a cautious *"Bonjour"* and turned away, but I was curious. I introduced myself as a *chasseur Americain*—an "American hunter"—figuring that that approach would break more ice than naming myself a tourist. Apparently, it worked.

"Did you see the boar, M'sieur?" the smaller one asked.

"The *boar?*"

"Yes . . . it came across the path just a moment ago."

His larger companion weighed in, "You can see its tracks in the mud, just back down the hill. I'll show you."

"We train our dogs in the summer . . . that's why we have no guns with us."

"My dog is a griffon. I don't think you have them in America."

"If you come up this time in the morning—maybe a little earlier—you will see many boars."

"We belong to the hunting society of Serignan. We operate waters for wildlife down in the valley. Have you seen them?"

"Would you like a picture of our dogs?"

"Would you like to join us for a *pastis* in Serignan this evening?"

"You should come back in the fall . . ."

■

In the next month I found tracks of boars, roe deer, and foxes; I saw many holes dug by truffle hunters, and one by a badger.

I walked in dry hills at once similar and strange, walked freely and without asking permission, just as I would in the public lands of New Mexico. Sometimes the dry heat, rocky ground, herbal smell, oaks and broom and pine, would make me feel I was exactly at home. The next moment a green lizard would appear, an improbable green-gold creature like a living bracelet, or a great brown jay with white flashes that resembled an oversize woodpecker, and I would know I was someplace very *other.* Sheep and goats and pigs, but no cows, grazed the pastures. Every evening, we drank or at least tasted six different Rhône wines. (One of my hosts was writing a book on the local wines.)

We ate wild boar and omelets freckled with truffles, both probably "harvested" within a mile of where we feasted. My hosts entreated me again and again to come back in the fall when the harvest and the game made the restaurants even better. I was promised such delicacies as thrush (now shot legally, carefully, in only two *departements* of France, unlike their still-wholesale destruction in neighboring Italy) and wild pigeon.

My hosts introduced me to a distinguished amateur entomologist, a self-described "rich peasant" who was a familial if not blood descendant of Fabre himself and a longtime correspondent with people like Nabokov. He showed me a letter in Fabre's own hand, written to his daughter on the death of her child; it was stained with her tears. The next day the curator of the Fabre "museum," his old house, showed us a letter—a fan letter!—from Darwin to Fabre.

I added approximately thirty birds to my life list, without even trying. Many of these were common town birds—jackdaws, turtledoves, screeching flocks of black swifts and white-bellied house martins that raced around the village at dusk. But high on the slopes of Mont Ventoux one afternoon soared a revolving silhouette that could have been a redtail at home but resolved itself into something unusual even in Provence: a Bonelli's eagle, a sort of giant goshawk of the open forests, that wheeled above the oaks for a moment before diving into a pine copse across the valley. Rarer quarry eluded me in the short time available. The gardener at Fabre's Harmas told me that I might find peregrines and even the legendary lammergeier, or bearded vulture, on the rocky slopes of the Dentelles, a bare limestone range that resembled uncannily the Sawtooths back home. I went once and saw only the ubiquitous magpies that swarm everywhere in Provence, rivaling the numbers seen in Bozeman, Montana, and providing another weird link with home.

Three more images, quickly: Every week we'd drive into the ancient Roman center of Orange for things we could not buy in the village. (We could buy more food in the village than in any comparable-size American town.) We'd enter under a Roman-built triumphal arch and drive past a Roman theater—an amphitheater built in the first century B.C. and still used for concerts.

One evening late in our stay we were eating in the courtyard. I heard the alarm calls of the jackdaws on the chimney and looked up to see not one but two great serpent eagles wheeling in stately majesty over the town, their white breasts reflecting the sunset as they soared over the screeching hordes of swifts.

And on the train home, somewhere down past Marseilles, I looked out the window to see a jeering magpie diving at a really startling bird of prey—fox red, yellow eyed, as fork tailed as a swallow. It was a red kite. Just a few hundred miles to the northwest, in Britain, it is considered that country's rarest bird.

I came home to the dirt roads of Magdalena, the five-hundred-inhabitant western town I have called home for fifteen years. Home to a book on golden eagles, which nest in the hills north of town, which really do (occasionally) kill a calf, which are still persecuted. Home to the new range wars, to the conflicts over use versus protection, public versus private, rancher versus "green," old-timer versus newcomer—conflicts that continue to divide my friends and everyone else who loves the West.

My cowboy friend Wade once dated a woman who lived in Paris, though Wade has never been very far east of the Rio Grande. (The West is more complex than coastal people often think.) He considers Europe one big paved snobbish expensive city, and he can't understand why anyone who lives on the edge of the Gila wilderness would want to go to France. His experiences with his friend, an Alabama-born pop singer who came here to shoot a music video, did nothing to change his mind. She complained about the dust, and, although she romanticized Native Americans, she didn't want to talk to them. She rambled on endlessly about what she could buy in Paris.

"Provence is different, you know," I said.

"Yeah, I guess," said Wade. "Sounds a little more like home. She said it's full of dirty peasants. I told her, what in hell did she think cowboys were?"

I liked the sound of that. "Exactly. Think of Magdalena with better food, great wine, Roman ruins, and houses from the twelfth century."

And then I laughed, amazed, because it was at least partly true. We have old villages, if not so old; ruins as old or older; fertile valleys; high dry mountains; houses not built of wood. One of our three languages has Roman roots. We have mule deer rather than roes, javelinas rather than boars. We still have bobcats and lions, while the Provençal lynx is merely a memory. Bears live rather closer to us than the Spanish border is to Provence, though our wolves—if they exist at all—are at least as far from us as the wolves in Alpine Italy are from Provence.

We are beginning to grow grapes for wine. Our eagles are, still, not so unexpected.

It is not popular to look to Europe for ideas on our ecological crises; far more so to blame it for them. This is particularly true of Mediterranean Europe, a dry and long-inhabited region that has been subject to everything from deforestation to songbird hunting. Northern Europeans from the Anglo-Saxon isles—Scandinavia, even Paris—love to blame the southerners for everything from polluting the ocean to decimating the migrant flocks of birds.

And yet I saw some things there that gave me hope, not just for Europe but also for the West, especially perhaps for my own *querencia* in the highlands of New Mexico . . . things I believe are not mere Mediterranean chauvinism. There is a spirit of localism there, of real "wise use" that includes stewardship, interactions, reverence, even the restoration of predators. (Not only the lammergeier and the Bonelli's eagle, but also the griffon vulture and the lynx are being restored in the south of France. All were persecuted less than a generation ago.)

The "natural" forests I saw on Mont Ventoux are not natural at all, but restored. According to the (excellent) English *Rough Guide to Provence*, "The deforestation dates from Roman times. In the nineteenth century it had got so bad that the entire mountain appeared shaved." Now the renewed woods are habitat for all the animals mentioned and more—owls, goshawks, vipers.

The hunting in southern France is interesting, too. It is one of the few places in Europe where the working class is still allowed and financially able to hunt. People like my friends on the hill band together into societies that lease and conserve land, private and public. There is easy access for nonhunters to the wild lands, unlike in Germany or parts of England. Even thrush hunting is now controlled; probably a better solution than in Italy, where everything is killed and nobody "on the ground" takes into account either local tradition or the necessity of protecting any species. The limited hunt in Provence satisfies the traditional hunters while protecting all but the commonest species, and even they are safe outside a few fall weeks. Most local observers agree that songbirds are returning, that I would have seen fewer ten years ago—this despite all the returning raptors!

The presence of game, including thrushes, in season does not seem to preclude a diverse ecosystem, human and nonhuman. I will not say "natural" and "unnatural"; the distinctions seem less obvious in the hills of the Vaucluse.

I don't want to be understood too quickly here, or give too much false comfort, or indicate solutions that are too easy. The Vaucluse, Provence as a whole, and the entire Mediterranean ecosystem have been used hard—perhaps too hard if such relative terms mean anything at all. There are species that have been destroyed and will never return. The Mediterranean itself has been used as a combination sewer-and-supermarket for too long. Gary Paul Nabhan, in his fine book *Songbirds, Truffles, and Wolves*, shows how alien species and greedy decisions have permanently altered the landscape in nearby Italy.

But for a tough place inhabited for thousands of years by Europeans, the hills of southern France give me hope: specifically, hope for New Mexico. It seems to me absurd to envision the practical protection of a place unless you plan to be around for two thousand years and more. Until this century, I doubt that most people in Provence, or in my ancestral Italian hills, thought of moving. Whether rich or poor, they were rooted. They had to care for the land they had as best they knew how, because they knew their children would be there after them. They were close to the sources of their food and water. It wasn't just that they couldn't move on; most preferred to stay. Many still do.

We know a little more now, and we are able to learn still more. We have new tools and methods of understanding. With them, maybe the present-day inhabitants of New Mexico could learn to live with our land with some of the grace and intimate interaction that the residents of the wilder parts of southern France seem to embody. I'd like to think of an agricultural ecology of wines and cheeses evolving — one that, as happens in all of southern Europe (and now California), recognizes the minute evolutionary differences between one hillside and another just a quarter mile away. Of course, we could also add chilis, beans, pigs, turkeys . . .

Why not have stone buildings that house generations of people?

I'd like to see hunters carefully husbanding all the local species, refraining from hunting them in bad years. I'd like to see them recognize that, cooked properly, a black-tailed jackrabbit or javelina is every bit as good (and worthy of reverence in the kitchen) as a European hare or wild boar. I'd like to see hunting continue to be available for the workers and natives, not just for rich urbanites who come for a week.

We could have an intricate mosaic of public and private lands, ranging from places of intense use to wilderness shrines. We still have space, and at least a little time.

We can keep our predators, rather than restore them; we have lost fewer species than Europe has. Within ten miles of my house in New Mexico live cougars, bobcats, black bears, two kinds of foxes, ringtails and badgers, goshawks, peregrines, prairie falcons, ferruginous hawks, and golden eagles. (We also have elk, mule deer, white-tailed deer, antelope, javelinas, turkeys, three kinds of quails, wild pigeons and doves, migrant geese, and cranes—more biological riches than Europe has seen since the Neolithic.) We are missing only wolves (maybe) and grizzlies; ironically, both hang on in relict populations near the edge of the Mediterranean.

What I am saying, finally, is that we need to meet a kind of challenge; we are overdue everywhere in North America. Here in my Southwest we need to admit that we human inhabitants—European Anglo, semi-European Latino, and "Native" (just an early bunch of immigrants, after all)—are here for the duration. Let us learn to grow good things appropriate to the region, build sturdy buildings, make delicious wine, and touch our environment (we cannot, after all, put it behind glass) in innovative, respectful, aesthetic, and sustainable ways.

You can—must—substitute your own area, animals, foods, ethnic groups here, whether you live in the Appalachians or the Cascades or the piney woods of Florida.

If we do all this, maybe a remote descendant, a visitor, might someday climb the Magdalena Mountains and see a great eagle—may *expect* to see it—soaring over a mountain forest, over elks and lions, finally drifting out over a valley of vineyards and chili fields and ancient buildings, where a river flows through gold ribbons of cottonwoods. Such a scene might be a measure of our adaptation to what we still insist on calling our "New" World.

Appalachia (1994)

PART II

Raptors

Eagles

A shadow falls across us, as silent as but swifter than a blowing cloud.

I should be ready. I know there is an eagle's nest tucked in a hole in the vertical wall above us. But the eagle's shadow falls on me as it must on a rabbit, on prey. I jump, involuntarily, and almost fall. Uncertain ankles can barely hold you upright on a cobbled bare slope of nearly forty-five degrees. The old female has bolted from an invisible perch where she must have been watching our antlike progress for at least half an hour. Now she stands on the wind, surveying us, not a hundred feet away. Her golden-naped head swivels but remains level, even when her outflung wings tilt and grab for purchase on the gusty spring wind.

If she is as sentient as I think she is she must recognize me. I have haunted this barren mountainside for fourteen years, hunting, collecting specimens, above all just watching. Nor does she have a large human cast with which to confuse me. People in my little outback town, five miles away by dirt road and rutted cattle track, have named the mountain "Titty" for the nipple-shaped fortress of vertical blocks that rise above its slopes, but they do not visit anything closer than the spring in the dry riverbed below. I've never seen a human on the slopes whom I didn't bring here myself.

She doesn't seem unduly alarmed, only cautious. She wheels, advances, so close now that I can see the glint in her mild brown eyes, and stands again in the wind, a little higher. Above and beyond, I can see the slighter form of her mate, always a little shyer, usually a little farther away. He faces the wind exactly parallel to her, as though they were two trout in a stream. Suddenly the string that tethers them to the mountain seems to break. They rise like two helium balloons. In seconds they are half a mile away, then more. They begin to wheel, move wings a little, and circle over the flat plain to the east, a silent sea of dead-grass brown. They hold their wings slightly above the horizontal, with a taut upward curve like that of the recurve bow, a tool invented by nomad horsemen who knew eagles. In less than a minute, they are out of unaided sight.

My companion sits down abruptly on the rocks and lights a cigarette. "That was impressive." She is looking at the empty sky, shaking her head. "I can't believe they were really there."

She is a city woman given to sardonic understatement, and does not gush about the wonders of nature; when, under my dubious influence, she bought her first bird guide, she wondered aloud if her brain was going soft. For a couple of months she has been driving down once a week from the city a hundred miles away to see new things. Once she demanded a bobcat, a creature I had never seen in the wild; that Sunday a diving raven pointed out our first, a feline the color of rock, with the bounding gait and fluffy coat of a rabbit, climbing a crack in a canyon wall. We have rolled up to sitting hawks on telephone poles and watched a buck antelope mount a doe, but this is the first time she has seemed moved. I watch her grin and blow smoke as she stares down the invisible track that the eagles left in the sky.

■

Falconry is older than our civilization by millennia. But the first falconers were practical. Such tribes as the Bedouin and the Kazakhs praise and prize their birds but scorn prey that is neither edible nor commercial. Eagles, with a greater need for food than small falcons, with life spans of thirty and forty years, must have paid their way. And yet: The oldest falconry cultures, the ones that seem to descend unbroken from the Neolithic, from the time when horses were tamed, are eagle cultures. It would make more metaphoric sense to speak of mankind, or at least Western man, riding out of the steppes of central Asia with an eagle perched before him in the saddle.

Once the eagle's shadow fell across all human societies. Eagles were big enough to be competitors, wise and bold enough to live close by unthreatened, and magical in their movement (". . . the way of an eagle in the air"). Almost every culture that left a written or pictorial record, from the ancient Greeks to the Japanese to the Aztecs, left a record of its eagle. The Aztecs knew and respected the aptly named harpy, the "snatcher." The Japanese in Hokkaido trained the swift mountain hawk eagle, calling it *kumataka*, "bear hawk," because it was strong enough to subdue foxes, raccoon dogs, and small deer.

But the eagle known to most old societies was the one that still lives on my mountain: the golden eagle, "the" eagle, *aetus*, the *Aquila* of the Romans, the "damn black Mexican eagle" of border sheepmen. Golden eagles, at least those of some races, are among the three or four largest predatory birds in the world, and are perhaps the most biologically successful. They live clear across North America, from Labrador to Mexico, in Siberia, across Asia to south of the Himalayas, through all of the Middle East and Europe, and down into the mountains of Morocco. Close relations inhabit South Africa and Australia. They are the bird of prey with the closest relations to humans, antagonistic, appreciative, utilitarian, mythical, real, and even theological, for uncounted thousands of years. Golden eagles are still actors in Pueblo Indian rituals; their tail feathers are sacred to the Plains tribes. The ancient Romans, who gave the name *Aquila* to the species and later to the genus, used them as war animals. They were reserved for emperors in European falconry, and are still used to hunt wolves in Kazakhstan and deer in eastern Europe. They have been poisoned by Scottish shepherds, accused of stealing babies, and hunted from single-engine airplanes in Texas as recently as the early sixties. Contrary to the assertions of some of their more sentimental defenders, they are capable of taking antelope and deer in the wild, and, at least once, have been proved to kill calves.

And they are old, old in a way that humans, evolutionary latecomers, can barely comprehend. They have seen human civilizations come and go, Yeats's "old civilizations put to the sword," and probably feasted on the remains, for eagles are not too proud to feast on others' meat. We don't know exactly how long *Aquila* has been around, but many modern bird families, near contemporaries, were already flying during the late Cretaceous, time of the tyrannosaur and triceratops.

Given the rarity of land-bird fossils (fragile hollow bones are evanescent to start with, and true eagles have always been inhabitants of windy uplands rather than the sediment-rich basins that produce fossils), it is likely that true eagles, identical to those alive today, were around to watch as we began to stand upright. Their shadows probably fell over the wandering bands of primates that exploded out of Africa less than a million years ago, long before those restless apes began to build such things as cities and civilizations. *Aquila* was always overhead, feasting on their leavings, nesting on the cliffs over their first river-valley fields.

■

Today, the twelfth of March, I climb the nose of the Magdalenas, eight miles south of the nest site of Titty, facing it across the westward extension of La Jencia Plain. When we were on the slopes of the eagles' mountain last week, I looked back to here across the intervening distance through my binoculars and saw a long horizontal crack in the rock a few thousand feet above the valley floor. As I have often flushed eagles from above that spot when walking the ridgeline, I though I might climb up and see, first, if they were adult-plumage eagles—without the white, black-tipped tail feathers beloved by Plains tribes that mark birds in the four or five years before they breed. If they were, they were probably "my" eagles; eight miles across these plains is no distance at all. People who live in densely populated environments, and travel mechanically, have no idea how large the world is and how small they are. At eight miles, you can see the nest clearly.

I walk and sometimes crawl with great effort up the north face. Eventually I arrive at a saddle, a confluence of great vertical Afghan knife ridges and yawning chasms, composed of rock, dirty snow, and a very few cholla and juniper bushes. It took me an hour to crawl to the first saddle, perhaps eighty-five hundred or nine thousand feet above sea level, two thousand or twenty-five hundred above the plain and the road. The forested top ridge is still a thousand feet above, and the ledge that I saw from Titty is inaccessible across a thousand-foot drop on another, slightly higher, ridge. The serrated ridges, scarred by vertical falls of rock and rectangular blocks, converge above me to the south. The light is gloomy, strained by a thunderous sky to the west, which is moving toward me. If it begins to blow or snow (which is predicted) this can be a terrifying place; there is no way to get down fast without wings. All the bare rocks move under my feet. As Jeffers said, it is "jagged country that nothing but a fallen meteor will ever plow; no horseman/Will ever ride there . . ."

The plain to the north, between me and the eagles' mountain, looks as flat and nappy as felt on a pool table; above that, but still below me, I can see the white spot of their droppings—actually they stain ten feet of ledge—without using my binoculars, although it is miles away. I raise my big 10X glasses to examine the plain. It is wrinkled and intricate around its edges, bare in the middle, and looks the way I imagine the bottom of the ocean would, if you took out all the water. Then, in the glasses, I discern a speck, a mote, an eyeball-floater out there, more than a mile away and well below me. It moves as steadily as though it were on rails, unlike the ubiquitous ravens that blow about and flap and dive. As it enlarges I know, before I can rationally describe any field marks, that it is the eagle, the female, and she's coming in. I have never seen her from above before. In mere seconds—remember, it took me an hour to climb a quarter mile—she is passing directly below me to my left, no more than a hundred feet away, on wings as steady as a mechanical glider's. It seems as though she moves by some strange invisible mechanical energy. I can see her mottled back and golden neck, a change from her usual shadow blackness. As she passes, she turns her head and looks at me—I can actually discern a flash, a reflection from her eyeball. Instantly she spreads her wings and wheels, catches the rising wind, and soars up past me as though she were on an elevator, turning to keep an eye on me. She keeps circling until she is level with the ledge across the chasm, perhaps five hundred feet above, then slides across in a single movement and furls her wings. I can just see her sitting there, alert but relaxed, with one foot drawn up.

■

Eagles are not much like us. The sentimental belief that an animal with whom we feel affinity is like us (or worse, *likes* us) is not the least of our cultural idiocies. It's probably easier to "understand"—all these questions and approximations must be put in quotes once you begin to think hard about them—an insect than an eagle. Insect senses and drives are far more alien, but their behaviors are reflexive and mechanical—binary, on or off. Eagles think and learn.

Our imagination fails to comprehend other animals in two ways. On the one hand, we dismiss them as a mass of insentient beings that react to stimuli and do not think, Cartesian automatons. On the other, we clothe human minds in different costumes, in feathers and fur and scales. We need new ways of imagining the minds of the "other bloods" with whom we share our world. Eagles contain power and intelligence in a body that weighs only twelve pounds. They can appear and disappear like magic in seconds, fall out of the sky at a hundred miles per hour to kill a hundred-pound antelope or a five-pound flying goose, with no tools, only the muscles of a hollow-boned body smaller than a child's. *Aquila*'s talons can exert a ton of pressure at their tips. Her great brown eyes, capable of resolving a pigeon's wing flick at two miles, weigh more than her intelligent brain.

Humans, not eagles, order experiences into stories. Nature has no plots, no ambitions, no internal conflicts; its endings are neither happy nor sad because its actors will not tell themselves stories the way we do. An eagle's perception of its own life would be of a bright eternal present like a carnivorous Buddhist's, confident, centered, and watchful, with a dim past and no thought of the future. Perhaps, it would be a bit like Ted Hughes's "Hawk Roosting": "I hold creation in my foot/Or fly up, and revolve it all slowly—I kill where I please because it is all mine . . . Nothing has changed since I began."

Too many writers who write about animals either pretend to scientific objectivity, using the passive voice and a deliberate flattening of affect to desiccate the subject on the page, or else anthropomorphize their protagonists. I believe, as I've already implied, that animals—birds and animals, anyway—do think, but that they think in ways that would seem alien and frightening to us if we could inhabit their minds. I said a moment ago that eagles have no story, but they do. It's just that their story is so different from ours that a narration of it would make no "sense." What to make of the mind of a creature that, if well fed, will sit from dawn to dusk just *watching*. Or to whom it is "moral" to kill her weaker sibling in the nest? Nobody but another eagle could easily read a lifelike narrative of an eagle's life without spasms of boredom or horror.

■

Because of the way they view the world, we do not "bother" eagles. But they do need what ecologists call a healthy prey base. A village and farm economy supports eagles very well if we do not persecute them too efficiently. My ancestors in the Italian Alps and Ireland and Scotland doubtless knew the golden eagle; *Aquila* still lives in all those places today. A few years ago, when I spent a month hiking around some obscure corners of northern Provence, I didn't expect to see eagles; the French are notorious for killing raptors. A nation of food-loving hunters with all the old-fashioned prejudices against predators, it only recently discovered that birds of prey are almost irrelevant to gamebird populations. But to my surprise, predatory birds considered rare in more conservation-minded parts of Europe were everywhere. Red kites soared over Roman ruins. Bonelli's eagles, close relative of the noble Japanese *kumataka*, wheeled in courtship flight over oak copses beneath the bare teeth of the Dentelles. Best of all, one pair of eagles would come to us. Every evening, as we ate our dinner in the courtyard of the presbytery in Serignan, two great snake-eating short-toed eagles, "*circaetes de Jean-le-Blanc*," would soar out over the village. They'd drift in high overhead, far above the wheeling screeching flocks of swifts that swirled around the town like rush-hour traffic, and turn around and around in stately majesty, flashing snowy undersides as they banked in the setting sun.

Eagle tolerance is not without limits, of course. A real modern city of tens of thousands and more paves over their food supply. I grew up in Boston and didn't know a life with eagles until I moved to rural New Mexico. Now if I want to I can see an eagle every day. In the winter we have many eagles; New Mexico is a wintering ground for goldens from as far away as Alaska. But we have breeding pairs, too; three pairs within twenty miles that I know. The nearest aerie is the one on Titty Mountain. These eagles are neighbors, if not exactly friends.

Eagles

■

Here are some of the things I have seen eagles do in the last few years, or that my neighbors have seen. Or that they think they have seen, for eagles seem to have the power to make people see things that are not so.

I'm coming down a narrow canyon late one afternoon, accompanied by a foxy little yellow mutt of local ancestry. She has the moves and habits of a wild dog, or as near to those as a domestic dog is ever likely to have: She pops into the air and comes down with forefeet and muzzle together to trap and eat a beetle or mouse, and has no patience with the less feral, slow-moving intellects of my bird dogs. Because of this she is a good collector-naturalist's companion, at least if I can get to whatever she has discovered before she has eaten it. She will never be bitten by a snake.

We are in an area of broadly separated oaks over deep grass when Winnie, who had been traveling ten feet to my left, suddenly shies and ducks between my legs, tail tucked in. I jump involuntarily; her movements signal fear before I can consciously formulate the thought. I look over my shoulder as a great moving shadow passes me at knee level, trailing a wing that all but brushes my leg. As my eyes focus the female eagle is already thirty feet ahead of me, climbing, looking back over her shoulder. I, who never sees the anger that many who don't live with raptors imagine on their "faces" (it's that bony sunshade over their eyes), suddenly imagine a passing malevolence in her gaze, like a shouted epithet. Winnie loses all sense and rushes downhill, barking at her assailant. But the eagle has missed and ignores her, sailing on down the valley, a hundred feet above its floor, rocking on the evening downdraft.

■

I'm driving up a long paved driveway toward a house outside the town, a prefab owned by the forest service. Its chief virtues are that it

45

is located two miles from town, and that a steep rock spire inhabited by banded rock rattlers and Mearns' quail rises just beyond its walled backyard, where I once flushed a mountain lion that was curious about my pigeons. It is sunset, just after a summer thunderstorm, and the spire glows an improbable orange-gold against a background of bruised sky, not unlike an *Arizona Highways* cover.

Three dots circling above the rock resolve themselves into a young eagle with snowy tail roots, and two barking ravens. Normally eagles treat ravens the way all predatory birds react to their avian tormentors: They ignore them as much as possible, while leaving with their dignity intact. Ravens are fliers of surpassing grace and daring; not even peregrine falcons seem to be able to catch or frighten them. The ravens call and dip as the eagle soars; then one, emboldened perhaps by the greater bird's forbearance, dives and seems to make momentary contact. As it dips below the eagle, she tucks a wing, rolls, and falls toward the raven. The raven takes in the situation before a human could react and flies straight at the ground, accelerating faster than gravity's pull. The eagle strokes once and falls like a thunderbolt, an inverted heart, a monster falcon. Although she does not flap once, she is overtaking the raven as they approach the clifftop. The raven — in a move that excites me to a cheer — flies within two feet of the rock, then makes an impossible right-angled turn and scrambles off through the air, screeching. The eagle, for all her greater speed, cannot maneuver in such close quarters. Her wings unfurl like a black explosion as she brakes and lands upon the ledge; that she can do this, rather than smash herself to bits, seems even more miraculous than the raven's turn.

She sits and glares for a moment, then turns to preen her shoulders. The ravens do not press their luck but drift off to the west, calling.

■

While I am still living at that house, I answer a honk in the driveway one day to see two ranch ladies in their seventies, whom I know from the local bar, sitting in a pickup. Mildred, the older, is businesslike: "We thought you ought to know. There's a big eagle up at the tank in Hop Canyon, and it's sick."

I'm a little amused, though I try not to let it show; I'm not used to older-generation ranchers being solicitous about "varmints." They tell me that it was "just sittin' on the ground" by the tank (a dirt stock pond) and that it "hopped away and looked at them," at which point they decided to drive the seven miles to my house.

When I arrive at the tank I pass a family of picnicking villagers (shady Hop Canyon, five miles south of town, is our best substitute for a park in the summer) but decide not to confuse things by questioning them. I find the "sick" eagle in a grove of oaks upcanyon from the tank, perched in the top of a ten-foot tree. Her belly feathers are still damp. She isn't sick; she has been bathing and is too waterlogged to get airborne. She is lucky to have met humans as well mannered as Aunt Bert and Mildred.

■

Eagles up close: I've handled one local bird, a huge old female of almost thirteen pounds. She had found her way into a steel trap. It was probably one set in a technically illegal manner, with some sort of visual lure, or perhaps a legal set placed under a thin cover of dirt beside a goat or sheep carcass left by coyotes. What I did know—her captors didn't speak English—is that she was caught on the Navajo reservation by relatives of a friend, and that my reputation as one who inexplicably likes birds probably saved her life. I arrived to find her sitting on the ground in a chicken coop, perfect but for one smashed toe as ugly and filthy as a cigar butt. When I crawled in, with gloves on both hands, she ignored me as much as possible. I trapped her feet with my hands and swung her up into my arms as though she were an enormous predatory baby. She remained calm. Unlike a grabby fish-eating bald eagle she never offered to bite me, even though her great

bill was inches from my nose. Understand: She might have, as a falconer would say, "footed" me, if she'd had the opportunity. But since
she couldn't, she neither struggled nor screeched, but waited and
watched. I transferred her to a dark box for her ride to the rehabbers
and out of my ken, and never saw her again, although I heard she
regained the sky three months later.

(Footing. The last eagle I handled before the Alamo Navajo
female was eighteen years previous . . . a "little"—six pounds—male
tawny eagle, a lesser Eurasian relative of the golden. Two years on con-
crete in a zoo had dulled his talons until they resembled knitting needles more than scimitars. When I swung him up onto my fist for the
first time, wearing a gauntlet so heavy I couldn't feel a hawk's grip
through it, he glared at me for a moment and then squeezed. In a
moment, pain like a drawn-out hammer blow knocked me to my
knees. My girlfriend found this hilarious. I sat on the grass and
moaned, then tried to be still. The eagle stared at me, mouth open.
He did not tighten his grip, because it was already as tight as it could
be, but he flexed it a little, left, right. I asked my friend to light me a
cigarette. I smoked unfiltered Camels then and still can feel the bite
of the smoke, the tears on my cheeks, the unbelievable—because
drawn out and unrelenting—pressure on my hand. Three cigarettes
later the eagle relented, drew in his foot, flapped up to his perch.
When I eased my hand out of the glove I could see no breaks in my
skin, only white spots. The emergency room doctor found a cracked
bone in the back of my hand, which had by then swollen as though I
had been bitten by a rattlesnake. It stayed black and purple for a
month.)

Legendary eagles exist, too. I live in a county where the only
instance of cattle (i.e., baby calf) predation by eagles ever accepted by
the Audubon Society took place. Those who understand eagles understand that *kill* does not mean "carry." An eagle has a hard time getting
airborne with a large jackrabbit. Yet I spent one night drinking whiskey

and trying to escape the descendant of a rancher (he was not a rancher himself, which may or may not be significant) who insisted on telling me that he had seen two eagles "fly off" with a four-hundred-pound steer the previous winter. That this would be the equivalent of his carrying away an eighteen-wheeler cattle truck did not seem like a diplomatic thing to say at the time.

■

I have seen eagles in odd habitats. The strangest space was probably that inhabited by a calm male, who perched on his handler's fist at the Explorers' Club banquet in Manhattan. All the other animals brought in to entertain the formally dressed throng seemed alien and uncomfortable. A python crawled continuously through a woman's arms like an animate Slinky bent on being somewhere else; a kestrel quivered in intense overstimulation, occasionally flipping over backward the length of his bootlace leash, beak open and panting. But the eagle surveyed the whole scene, blinking, yawning, sometimes standing on a single foot. Once or twice he even "roused"—expanded all his feathers, then shook them down—the surest sign that a bird is comfortable.

But the eagles I remember with the most pleasure were doing nothing at all other than, of course, being eagles. We were coming up the hill from the Rio Grande valley one evening when my companion pointed wordlessly out the window. I pulled over, seeing moving dots like fighter planes in my peripheral vision. When I got out and trained my glasses on them the optics revealed the local pair, the Titty Mountain eagles, flying or rather gliding wing to wing like two yoked Piper Cubs. They were just above us and moving very fast, although their bodies were as rigid and motionless as those of two sailplanes. They moved as though propelled by some invisible but potent force until they drew even with the bare top of a little volcanic hill just south of the road. First one, then the other, unfurled wings, stopped, dropped, landed. They turned their raised heads toward each other for a moment as though in acknowledgment, then arranged themselves facing west as though to watch the sunset. I very nearly cheered.

I am human, and so wish I could fly with eagles, hunt with them like an earthbound mate, thinking and imagining myself blowing down the wind like a shadow on furled wings, falling from the sky like a sentient thunderbolt to kill with my hands and mouth. This wish, to understand, to know, and even to be for a moment something different—or, failing that, to speak of it—is an entirely human wish; an eagle would not comprehend, or care.

California Falconers' Journal (1995)

Why I Love Goshawks

They are everywhere, but you don't see them. Their nests are in the mountains, in tall pines; or sometimes in aspens, in little watered valleys high up, in grizzly habitat where it's always cool. If you are looking for a little native trout rather than the big selective browns of the tourist streams, you may enter the goshawk's nesting territory. She'll let you know. Your first clue will be a sudden loud birdcall: "KUKUKUKUK!" Next you'll see a huge gray hawk stroking under the canopy, twisting and turning, crying as she flies. She seems too big to fly so fast in such close cover. If you don't retreat, she'll fly closer, screaming outrage. Maybe you'll hear her mate join in with a higher-pitched version of her cry: "KIKIKIKIK!" Like all male birds of prey he is smaller, slighter than she is; he'll rarely come close.

While she may just come up behind and hit you on the head. She's the only raptor in America that is likely to do that. Even golden eagles slink away. Female goshawks will rip your scalp, grab your shirt; they'll even bounce off your motorcycle helmet. Trail bikes don't intimidate them—though they can frighten horses. Unless you're a hard-core falconer, and a goshawk fanatic at that, you'd best avoid a nest full of young goshawks.

Outside nesting territory goshawks are wraiths, forest ghosts. The old birds—with blue backs, silver fronts, red eyes—are hardest to see. The brown first-year birds are bolder. They have not learned all their tricks yet, nor do they hold territory; they come down onto the plains, haunt river valleys and coulees. If you are hunting winter pheasants in the heavy undergrowth along a creek out by Grassrange, or along the upper Madison, you may come around a corner of brush in the late afternoon to see a big young female gos sitting in the top of a willow, at eye level, no more than thirty feet away. Her streaked buffy breast glows in the bloody light; her eyes, still the pale yellow of youth, are on yours. She's waiting for you to flush a bird for her; using you, quite consciously, as her dog. We are not used to such arrogance. I suspect a lot of goshawks still lose their lives at this moment.

I first came to know goshawks in New England, close to thirty years ago. My friends and I were a hard-core, scruffy bunch of hunter-gatherers; students, Vietnam vets, blue-collar workers, woods hippies. We were hungry and fierce and wild and poor. We drank prodigious amounts of whiskey and beer, smoked like chimneys, and could still run uphill on snowshoes. Many of us were falconers. Although we romanticized the nearly vanished peregrine, our real icon was the goshawk. No other bird could fly so well and fast in those enclosed fields and industrial parks, even golf courses. No other bird thrived at twenty below. And nothing else, neither the steady but slow redtail nor the noble falcons, could take the range of prey that goshawks could: snowshoe hares, ducks, pheasants, quail, not to mention the occasional stray cat, green heron, or marsh hawk. A goshawk's ambition knows no bounds; I once saw one ride a flushed Nantucket white-tail doe for about six bounds, then return as though puzzled that she couldn't hold the huge rabbit. It was not an accident that the old French peasant falconers called the gos *cuisinier*: "the cook." You could easily catch most of your meat ration for the winter with a gos: a hundred rabbits, twenty ducks, a few "miscellaneous."

Of course you also had to put up with goshawk temperament. My first one, an exceptionally ferocious young male, almost drove me mad. He was as likely to attack me, my dog, a harrier, or a green heron as he was to chase legitimate quarry. I let him go. Later he became the protagonist of the first piece I sold to a major magazine, about how crazy he and other goshawks were. Still, I don't agree with the yuppie falconer who looked at my gos a while back and alleged that he had had "one of those, *once.*" He preferred expensive, sweet-natured, domestic-bred falcons, peregrines and gyrfalcons. Now that these are available hardly anyone in the United States flies goshawks. It's not that they are vicious or, as kids I know say, "mean." They are simply alien. As I said in a book a number of years ago, "They are aloof, brooding, schizoid predators, difficult to train, delicate and murderous, prone to strokes, fits, and lung disease. They are rarely affectionate. Their capacity for ignoring the falconer is unmatched. They fear strange people, dogs, cats, and phantoms."

Then, of course, they go out and catch you your winter meat. And grab onto deer.

Obviously, humans and goshawks must work to understand each other, but this is hardly a measure of success for either. These days I feel less like metaphorizing the gos in quite so many anthropomorphic terms: *vicious, aloof, brooding, murderous.* In fact she may be one of the most successful predators on earth. Only the peregrine is found on more continents, but she is confined to cliffs over water, while the gos lives anywhere in the Northern Hemisphere where there are forests.

When I moved West in the late seventies I found goshawks everywhere. In winter, high in the Shoshone Range of northern Nevada, I watched a big, young female work a contour around a sage-covered slope, beating, flapping, gliding, and turning, while the chukars around me ceased calling and seemed to hold their breath. I could have seen a virtually identical picture in Afghanistan. When I settled in New Mexico I soon found goshawks there, nesting in the piney mountains less than ten miles from my house. My first glimpse was of a little blue male, chasing a bandtail pigeon down a narrow canyon, twisting and turning through the piñons, skidding on the curves. He must have been in sight for at least ten seconds. But the glimpse revealed their habitat, and I found myself playing hot and cold with them once again, listening for that wild cry of alarm. A few years later I found my first pair in the mountains of southwestern Montana. They attacked us on our way in to see a new peregrine aerie. Goshawks have never needed to be restocked.

In fact, they are the commonest and most successful member of the genus *Accipiter*, the "true" hawks. They live in Montana, New Mexico, and everywhere between, with a few extending down into the Sierra Madre of Old Mexico. They live in Maine, Massachusetts, and New York, down into Virginia, and perhaps farther South; they are expanding, or reclaiming, their range in the East. They are found across the northern tier of the United States, wherever there is forest—in the Pacific Northwest, north to Alaska, and to the tree line across Canada. They are also present from England to Japan, across the whole enormous forested bulk of northern Eurasia, south to the Atlas Mountains of Morocco and the Himalayas of northern India and Nepal. Extremely close relatives inhabit Madagascar and New Guinea. Recently a few activists have alleged that *Accipiter gentilis*, the northern goshawk, is endangered by the logging of old-growth forest. This could be a dangerous strategy, one that achieves the opposite of what its supporters hope. There are necessary, ample reasons to defend old-growth forest on its own merits, but goshawks, however seldom seen, are far from rare. Even on the southern fringes of their range, where their numbers fluctuate with drought, I've been able to find nests. In the North they are probably at saturation whenever there's suitable habitat; "invasions" from Canada allowed them to reinhabit the East when the forest came back, as they are now reinhabiting the British Isles.

These days, after years of dalliance with falcons, I'm flying a gos again. Sara is a big female, five years old, from the Wind River Range in Wyoming. She was a gift from Danny, who has moved on to a male golden eagle; another whole story.

She is . . . fair, but not exactly friendly. She'll come calmly enough to your hand, for food or just because she's been called, but she doesn't hang around long for no reason. She'll turn her head upside down in affectionate greeting if you pass, but she'll not suffer much familiarity.

She also has a goshawk's tendency to grab. I long ago stopped waving my ungloved right hand around where goshawks could grab it, having once watched my calm mentor in falconry, Ralph Buscemi, stand "handcuffed" by a nervous male for over half an hour during a hunt. Falcons don't *do* this. I keep my right hand below the other, and watch my fingers. I tell my partner, Libby, and stepson, Jackson, that they are getting an early Ph.D. in hawk handling.

So, well, why? Peregrines are "nice," sweet, as affectionate as dogs, and get good press. They are really falcons; you don't have to explain that yes, you are a falconer, but no, this is not a falcon. They are elegant, feminine, with big black spaniel eyes. The goshawk is beautiful, too, but in a scary way. Her bony-browed eyes ("what but fear/Winged the birds . . . and jeweled with such eyes/The great goshawk's head," as Jeffers wrote) look like cups of blood. Her great curved talons can press thousands of pounds at their points, sometimes right through your glove.

And yet I came back to her, my first love among birds. I am an itinerant and, as a hunter, a generalist. I live in several places; my dog is a springer spaniel, my gun a 16 gauge; no specialist among us. I chase Mexican quail and Montana grouse, pheasants and ducks, jackrabbits and snipe, cook and eat them all with relish and happy greed and I hope a little grace. I too am a bit of a peasant, and a *cuisinier*. We all work well together.

Besides, I find her lowered head, heavy shoulders, great sickle-tipped hands, fierce white eyebrows, bloody eyes, eagle's beak, blue back, and soft silver underbelly express a harder, more austere beauty than the easy prettiness of the peregrine. The Japanese, with their strange combination of ferocity, aesthetics, and pragmatism, knew this. One of the commonest themes for decorating the *Tsuba*, or Samurai sword-guard, is a tiny goshawk, perhaps three-quarters of an inch high, with inlaid gold for its feet and beak and eyes. Their seventeenth-century paintings of trained goshawks are among the most exquisite biomorphic works of art in existence. Sometimes I think I must have one tattooed on my left, falconer's arm.

Hunting with a gos is elemental, primitive, direct. It does not take elaborate setting up, teams of dogs, training flights, or electronics. I prefer old-fashioned—that is, pre-1800, pre–Industrial Revolution— flights. I like flights "out-of-the-hood" at opportunistic quarry better than organized game—hawking for pheasants. I prefer wild country to game farms, walking to sitting in a blind, spaniels and greyhounds to pointers. I love to see a peregrine stoop, whether at a sky trial or over a brace of pointers; such a feat is very much an art, and just a bit artificial. Hunting should never get too far from chasing, gathering, eating.

Or wildness. My old mentor, Ralph, now lives in Sheridan, where he moved for trout and hawks. He was once trained by a pair of goshawks to throw them pigeons; sometimes the bolder female would come down, hover, and take one from his hand. He has movies. No other wild hawk would do that. You'd only need to take one more step. As Ralph says: "If I could get 'em to follow me into the woods, I could give up the rest of it."

Big Sky Journal (1996)

The North-of-the-Waste White

The goshawk has always been the bird of choice among pragmatic falconers. Forget the romantic image of the nobleman with the peregrine on his fist; despite Roger Tory Peterson's vivid comment about mankind emerging from the mists of prehistory "with a peregrine falcon perched on his fist," the first falconers were practical. The sweet elegant peregrine is a toy for developed civilizations, as useful as a thoroughbred or an opera. In medieval Europe, the nobles flew peregrines and Arctic gyrfalcons at such utterly impractical quarries as carrion-eating kites and herons. Most of the herons brought down were released minus one head plume and with the added weight of an inscribed silver ring on the leg; the similarity to the favorite "blood" sport of today's leisure class, catch-and-release fly fishing, is almost too obvious. The older falconry societies scorn such effete refinements. The oil-rich sheiks of the Middle East don't *need* the quarry that their hawks bring down but still hunt in the hungry headlong way that was bequeathed to them by their nomadic ancestors. They chase hares, houbaras, and stone curlews: traditional food animals. Eagles, big enough to injure their trainers and with a greater need for food than the small falcons, must have paid their way. And yet the falconry tribes with the longest unbroken traditions, the Kazakhs and Kirghiz, fly eagles and goshawks.

My bird these days, Sara, is five years old and weighs forty ounces. She has eyes like dark rubies, a slate blue back, a silver breast like the hair of a dark handsome woman in middle age. Her feet are disproportionately large and stout, like a small eagle's; her inner talon, decurved, razor edged, black as a cape buffalo's horn, is over an inch long. She takes on an average of sixty-five head of game a year, from partridge to jackrabbits, and is better at what she does than I will ever be at what I do.

Sometimes I'll see a reflection on the window of a car as I go out with Sara. Being a writer, and so too much of a romantic, I'll stop to look at the picture that her controlled ferocity and austere beauty makes on my hand. At such times I'm likely to think suddenly of another picture and wonder, ruefully, if I could ever live up to the standards of its subjects.

This one is from a coffee-table book, *A Day in the Life of the Soviet Union*. It shows a spare, ancient, elegant old man astride a tall "modern" horse. The caption informs us that he is Turdy Adiev from the Fergana Valley in Kirghizia. He wears a long wool frock coat, a double-breasted striped jacket, a white shirt without a tie buttoned at his neck, and a round wool skullcap sectioned like an orange. His face is that of a Chinese sage but browned by the elements, contrasting with his curved white mustache and neat chin beard. He's surrounded by tall birch trunks, dappled by their leaky shade. On his fist perches a huge white goshawk with glaring yellow eyes.

■

The goshawks from Siberia and the Altai, legend tells us, are white. A nineteenth-century treatise, the *Baz-Nama y Nasiri*, said that white goshawks came from "Turkestan," which at the time meant any-

58

thing between Persia and Mongolia, and added, "The female of this variety . . . is noted for its large size." A Chinese hawk-training manual from the same period, *The Divisions of the Predators of the Flesh*, speaks of a bird called the "North-of-the-Waste White" and says of it that "its body is long and large . . . it is foremost among the goshawks." The Japanese, who revere goshawks the way Western nobility did peregrine falcons, made them one of the theme birds of classical painting—although Western catalogs always, maddeningly, refer to the subjects of these paintings as falcons or even *peregrine* falcons. (Like most practical Asian falconry cultures, the Japanese mix pragmatism and aesthetics—and have a poorer class who pursue foxes and martens with eagles called *kumatakas*: "bear hawks." All these are totemic Japanese animals.) In 1971, researching seventeenth-century "falcon" art in the basement of the Museum of Fine Arts in Boston, I came across a six-paneled, seven-foot-high silkscreen bearing six life-size goshawk images in sepia ink. Each one shows a different plumage or age: brown-streaked juveniles, adults with fierce white eyebrows and bared breasts, all on tall perches and tied to embroidered screens, with ornately knotted braided cords.

The last bird was different. She was larger than the rest, paler eyed, and white. Only a lattice of ghostly pale brown feather edges, like sun-faded ink, marred her snowy shoulders. At the time I had never heard of such a thing as a white goshawk and wondered if she might be some kind of albino.

Over the next twenty years I learned a little more. Like the legendary and scientifically mysterious Altai gyrfalcon, the only bird for which Arab princes will actually pay five-figure prices and which is therefore never allowed to fall into the hands of infidels, white goshawks are too valuable and useful to find their way to the West. A few stories drifted out of the eastern fringes of Russia and old documents, but until the fall of the Soviet Union such birds remained in the East, locked behind the old "Iron Curtain."

They are not albinos: They are *albidus*; *Accipiter gentilis albidus* to be exact, the largest race of the goshawk. Their exact range remains mysterious, but like many circumpolar winged predators, they erupt south in lean food years and turn up in strange places. In 1991 my friend Dan, an accomplished falconer, caught one in downtown Rock Springs, Wyoming.

■

Rock Springs is the kind of town in which postmodern directors set nouveau-noir films. Its setting, amid sagebrush flats and eroded buttes, between some of the longest straight stretches of highway in the United States, is too stark for most tastes; coming or going, you don't pass any trees for hours, only mining scars and antelope. The nearest city is Salt Lake, and it's four hours of over-the-speed-limit travel away. Its architecture has been called "postnuclear" by somebody who likes it. Rock Springs's population and trailer parks swelled during the oil boom, along with bumper stickers saying OIL FIELD TRASH AND PROUD OF IT, then dwindled, leaving a legacy of unemployment and despair. Its radio stations play more sixties rock than anyplace I've ever been. It is surrounded by named dirt paths announced by freeway signs, like WAGONHOUND ROAD. It is neither chic nor nouveau West.

I love the place. Rock Springs is the capital of the Red Desert, land of freeze-dry and burn, the capital of antelope and eagle and sage grouse and tough funny survivors. It will be the last western town that succumbs to yuppies. But the treeless, wind-blasted winter void is a hell of a place to find a goshawk hatched in a fir tree in Siberia.

Of course, maybe a city, even a little one, looks more like a forest than the plains surrounding it. It was a downtown resident who called Danny that cold November day and reported a "gyrfalcon" in his backyard. Danny showed up minutes later with hawk bait—a common pigeon—wearing a leather jacket covered with running nooses of monofilament fishing line, dragging a light anchor made of a piece of dowel. In theory, the hawk could grab the pigeon, become entangled in the nooses (the pigeon would usually escape unharmed, protected by its leather shield), and then be unable to fly away because of the dangling weight of the stick below.

Danny looked into the backyard through the window. Perched in a bare apple tree, facing away from him, was a huge white hawk. "First I thought, 'Yeah, it's a gyr.'" Gyrfalcons are never common, and always exciting, but can be seen regularly on the plains of Montana and Wyoming in the winter. However, the ones that come south into this region are usually gray or brown or silver, not white. "I kept staring at her—something was weird. Then she wagged her tail sideways—you know, like a gos. And I said to myself, 'Holy shit, it's a white gos!'"

Goshawks are common in the mountains of Wyoming, but western gosses are smaller birds, brown when young, gray when adult, like Sara. They have red eyes. This one turned and looked straight at the window. "And it had these *fluorescent* gold eyes. That's when I knew it wasn't an albino—it was *albidus!*" He pitched the pigeon out through the window and the white hawk fell out of the tree onto it as though she had been a restaurant patron impatiently waiting for a meal. Seconds later, Dan was holding the Siberian immigrant in his hands.

And was faced with a quandary.

Falconry may be more regulated now than in medieval times, when it often meant heavy punishment for a commoner to so much as restrain a noble falcon. Those of us who came to falconry in the sixties and seventies imbibed a fair amount of the paranoia that was in the air then and tended to incline toward not just prudence but also invisibility. Back then, sportsmen shot hawks even as DDT thinned their numbers and bureaucrats banned their possession. Things are much better now, but there is still enough paper required on hawks, both state and federal, to make record keeping a problem. Dan had a permit to catch a goshawk, but not a Siberian goshawk. After weighing her (she weighed an astonishing fifty-nine ounces, as opposed to forty for Sara), he took her out of town and let her go.

He's still outraged at what he considers the dumbest mistake of his life. "Three weeks later I get a call about a big white hawk that's sick, down by the railroad bridge. I go down and it's her, just sitting on the ground. But she still comes in to the pigeon. I can tell she's sick. She's wheezing and there's this foam around her nostrils. I pry open her beak and there's all this cheesy stuff. She had a mega-attack of frounce." Frounce, a trichomonad, is present in most pigeon populations. Though it doesn't often affect them visibly, it can be virulent in birds of prey, especially goshawks. The weakened bird's weight had dropped to twenty-nine ounces, and the keelbone along her breast felt like a hollow-ground knife blade with feathers. Twenty-four hours later, despite heat and medicine and Danny's expert nursing, she was dead. He called the Smithsonian, which sent a special courier to Rock Springs to pick up the carcass of the first *Accipiter gentilis albidus* ever recorded on the North American continent. Before the courier arrived, Danny pulled two secondary feathers. He kept one, and gave the other one to me. It is snow white with just the remotest watermark of pale brown barring. I use it as a bookmark, keeping it in the page of the *Handbook of North American Birds* that refers to goshawk species.

Published privately (1994)

Lost Partner

Don't ever get a goshawk angry after she has eaten, at least not unless you have a secure hold on her jesses.

You'd think that anyone who had hunted with hawks for more than thirty years would know this on a level akin to instinct. T. H. White once said, "The thing about being associated with a hawk is that you can never be slipshod about it." But Sara was always a "good" gos. She didn't show the happy doglike affection of a true falcon or possess the essential calm of a buteo or eagle, but she was always fair and seldom temperamental. At least not until something annoyed her.

The "something" this time was so trivial that it could only irritate a creature as alien as an accipitrine hawk: I had fiddled with her feet, trying to rearrange the jesses in order to hook them to the leash, before she was ready. She cackled, stomped, shifted, flapped, and tugged; the greasy straps slipped through my fingers. If she had flown to a tree we might have negotiated; I might have at least called her down to the lure, the padded bird-shaped flat that falconers swing and throw to toll in their birds from far away. But she mounted up and headed west at full speed, to disappear into a freshening blizzard.

Humans are the only animals who give their hearts to other species. Some of these will respond. If you love a dog, a dog will love you back. The loss of a dog, in the field or even to old age, can be almost like the loss of a mate or a child.

Twice in the last twenty years I have had dogs "run away." The first time, Maggie, my old spaniel matriarch, and her daughter, Sassy, chased a bunch of turkey poults away from the base of a fire tower and disappeared into New Mexico's Apache Kid Wilderness for the better part of the week. I remember it as the second worst bereavement of my life, and am not ashamed to admit that I cried in relief when we picked up the dogs seven days later. The other time, I was boarding Sass and Bart—he's still around at thirteen—with a friend on the Navajo reservation while I flew back East to attend to business. They broke out and roamed the res for ten days.

Point is: They were looking for me. And when Maggie and Sassy got lost from the tower, they kept returning. As the books tell you to do, I left a coat on the ground by the tower. Both dogs, three days apart, were curled up on it when we drove up out of the morning mists. It's hard to lose a dog.

You cannot say this about even the most affectionate hawk, never mind the aloof and self-contained gos. It's fatally easy to lose birds, even with telemetry. Nowadays all the big "longwings," the true falcons that may kill miles away if they get in a tailchase, wear little transmitters about the size of a cigarette filter on their legs or tails. These have a line-of-sight reception distance of up to twelve miles. If an eagle or great horned owl doesn't eat your bird, you'll probably pick her up the next day, at the latest. But the gos is a short-distance bird, an avian shotgun, and so, like many traditionalists, I never outfitted mine with electronics. In hindsight, this was a very big, dumb mistake.

The first feeling is pure shock: "I-don't-believe-it." The second thought is the idiotic one that if you just run far enough in the direction in which the hawk has disappeared, you will find her sitting in a tree, waiting. I did, and I didn't.

Then you feel stupid. You do not—at least I did not—feel bereft, grieving, as you do when a beloved dog is lost. After all, if you are any good as a falconer the bird is going to survive, even prosper. Her business is hunting, and she's so good at it that one friend of mine calls falconers and houndsmen "accessories to the hunt." You feel dumb, as though you had just left the Purdey on the roof of the car and driven away.

And then you get determined. Birds of prey do not, as popular wisdom has it, "revert," at least not swiftly. They may not home (although some falcons will), but they will be perfectly happy to see you if you can just think enough like a hawk to appear where they are. I thought: food, trees, food. It was midwinter, and I figured that the banks of Sourdough Creek, with their big trees and feral ducks, were a likely possibility, especially because they also harbored rabbits and flocks of pigeons. So every day at dawn I'd hike the trail along the stream, calling, whistling, and swinging the lure. At dusk I'd skirt the black shadows on the edge of the cemetery above Peet's Hill, where congregations of corvids roosted. I'd swing the lure until sunset. It must be the loneliest scene on earth, one I've acted in more than once: a falconer staring into the west, twirling the lure around his head, and blowing on his whistle until the light is gone.

A week later, I hadn't seen or heard a thing. The word was out on the grapevine, to falconers and vets and raptor rehabbers. But not even the news I most dreaded—that Sara had been killed or injured attacking poultry or pigeons—had come in. I persisted in my actions, but with little hope.

About that time, a rancher ten miles west of town saw a big bird flying up into his open pole barn. Apparently Sara had no trouble killing for her food (there were ducks nearby) but sensibly preferred the accustomed safety of a roof overhead to the owl-haunted groves along the stream. The rancher called Fish and Game to report a "trained falcon." Fish and Game called the raptor biologist and eagle expert Al Harmata. Al poked his head around the door corner, saw the jessed gos, and substituted his glove, garnished with a piece of meat, for his head. Sara dove to his fist as though this was the intentional end to her escapade, and that was that.

The next evening I went to pick her up at the house of a mutual friend, a falconer. She was perched, hooded, on the stair rail as I entered. I picked her up, unhooded her, and stared into her utterly indifferent, blood red eyes. And I wondered, not for the first time, why hunters, so often damned in the postmodern world for cruelty, give their hearts to their hawks, and dogs, and horses, and other partners, again, and again, and again.

Big Sky Journal (1996)

Grouse Camp

A t the end of the long season, sometimes soon after Christmas or, if the going has been good, as late as February, a band of nomads gathers on the plains south of Portales, New Mexico, just west of the Texas border. Jim Weaver plays host. Once the first among equals and the greatest wanderer of all, one whose work and passions took him to the rivers of Greenland and the cliffs over the Zambezi, he is now more or less settled on a few sections of prairie near the one-building town of Pep.

Dan O'Brien, novelist, endangered-species biologist, and South Dakota rancher, has a little adobe house a couple of miles up a rutted dirt track from Weaver's. Its walled yard is pierced by a traditional western gate of black wrought iron, but with unusual design elements: A hawk hangs from its arched top bar, and across the bottom parade a pointing dog, a yucca, a three-dimensional cholla, a quail, and a dancing prairie chicken.

Kent Carnie's old silver Airstream trailer may be parked in a pasture nearby, if the snows of Montana and Wyoming have finally chased him south. A retired colonel in intelligence and a wildlife biologist, a student at Berkeley under Aldo Leopold's son Starker in the fifties, Kent has also traveled widely. He has banded birds on the frontiers of

Turkey and the Soviet Union and hunted the moors of Scotland, but now these ocean-flat fields hold one of his permanent camps.

Usually Tom Cade will show up at this time of year, with various flying partners in tow. A short, balding, affable man, he could as easily be a local rancher, at least until he begins to tell his traveler's tales: In fact, he was born on the New Mexico prairie. Since then he has studied shrikes in Alaska and eagles in Africa. He became a professor and perhaps the greatest living authority on the falcons of the world at Cornell, where in 1969 he began the project of breeding the peregrine falcon to introduce it back into the wild—a project many doubted could ever be accomplished.

In fact, what has brought these people to the plains is what Thomas McGuane, speaking in a rather different context, called "not even a mammal"; in fact, a bird. Or, actually, two kinds of birds—falcons and prairie chickens. For these are the men who brought back the peregrine falcon, and the prairies of the New Mexico–Texas border are the southern terminus of what the nomads call (proper noun here) Grouse Camp. They, and a few others who spend a little less time, have been working their way south through the grasslands and sagebrush basins since August, chasing what might be, if only for an ephemeral moment, the finest field sport that has ever existed on the planet.

■

High-end falconry is the strangest of all sports and, despite outsiders' perceptions, perhaps the humblest rather than the most arrogant. The process of learning takes the novice through a grueling apprenticeship and a Byzantine labyrinth of federal restrictions, the end result of which is that he learns to be polite to a bird whose eyes weigh more than its brain. Which is not to belittle it. A large falcon—a peregrine or gyrfalcon—is one of evolution's most perfect productions, a playful predator that lives to fly rather than one that flies to live, a bird that will harass flocks of smaller birds for the sheer hell of it and buzz its human and canine servants out of exuberance rather than aggression.

There is something addictive about the companionship of big raptors. You are often asked how you teach a hawk to kill. The simple answer is that you don't; it already knows how to do that better than you do. What you teach it is to return to you if it doesn't catch its prey, and to allow you to share the quarry if it does. With a wild-caught bird you do this by showing it that you provide food (not, incidentally, by "starving" it). Falcons, like all predators, are great opportunists and quick learners. Once they learn that your presence increases their chances of getting a meal, whether on the wing or directly from you, they'll quickly alter their behavior.

Most of the birds flown on the grouse plains are "captive" bred. I set off "captive" like this because "domestic" is probably a better word for them; often they are second generation or better, though human breeding of hawks in any numbers has only been going on for about twenty-five years. These birds are not just tolerant or opportunistic but positively affectionate. They will extend their heads forward for the hood, that little eyeless cap that falcons wear to prevent travel stress, as though to say, "Don't distract me with all that." They'll hold up their beaks to be cleaned after a meal. Some even fall in love with their owners—or, to put it more scientifically, imprint on them sexually. This can be an advantage if you intend to breed them by artificial insemination, but holds a lot of potential for embarrassment. In the spring imprinted birds can be possessive and loud.

Both the bird's opportunism and its affection contribute to the appeal of falconry. Tom Cade once called the sport an advanced form of bird-watching and he was exactly right. In falconry you get to watch, again and again, the kind of behavior that you might otherwise see once or twice in a lifetime. Then you get to call the bird out of the sky.

This magic exists in all falconry, even that practiced with such common "humble" birds as redtails and kestrels. But with peerless top-of-the-food-chain high fliers like peregrines and gyrfalcons it reaches its zenith. Such birds deign to catch only aerial prey (well, in theory, anyway—the Arctic gyrfalcon, living in one of the earth's most hostile environments, does not scorn "fur" if no flying food is available), and can dive to meet it at speeds in excess of two hundred miles per hour.

The gyrfalcon, a burly bird of variable coloration ranging from ice white to sooty black, can and will chase down anything that flies if it has to go twelve miles to do it. The peregrine, on the other hand, is an inhabitant of river valleys and other more enclosed areas. Its specialty is to "wait on," circling high above a likely spot until something desirable flies below it, at which point it folds its wings and falls. Gyrs can climb faster and straighter than peregrines, but often prefer to buzz around at low levels, content in the knowledge that no matter where the prey flushes, they can catch up.

Both methods have their advantages for the birds, though obviously the gyrs' can pose difficulty for the falconer. Falcons and hawks do not usually carry large prey, but wait where it has fallen; if they finish their meal before their human partner finds them, they may go aloft to find him or roost in a tree to sleep it off. But they don't have the directional sense of a homing pigeon. Modern falconers have dealt with the problem by developing telemetry. Each hawk is fitted with a transmitter about the size of a cigarette filter, tailing a soft silvery braid of antenna. Theoretically, if your bird flies out of sight you can track it down with a receiver and directional antenna. The system isn't foolproof, but it's a lot better than nothing. Before telemetry, more hawks were "lost" than lived out their lives in partnership with humans.

The falconer's other solution is to cross the gyr with the peregrine. Birds of the genus *Falco* have, like dogs and wolves, the ability to make many fertile crosses. The result is a sort of domestic superhawk that combines the virtues of the gyr and the peregrine, being big and fast enough to catch quarry the peregrine cannot handle but possessing the tendency to climb, wait, and "stoop," or dive. Such birds are also startlingly handsome, with the gyr's broad shoulders, heft, and variable colors, and the peregrine's hard slick feathers and military markings.

■

When I first heard about hybrid falcons, in the early eighties, I was intrigued but dubious. Biologically, I was fascinated; the idea of fertile interspecies hybrids and domestic falcons was food and drink to someone who almost became an ornithologist, and who still attempted to keep up with the literature. As a falconer, I was less impressed. I had grown up with goshawks and redtails in the pastures of the Northeast. Before the late seventies, the English were considered the elite of hawking; they flew peregrines at red grouse, a form of ptarmigan, in the Scottish Highlands. I believed what an English friend had written me: How could man be arrogant enough to imagine that he could improve upon nature?

But rumors continued to reach me from the West—of gyrfalcons, scorned by the English but treasured by a new breed of American fanatics; of flights at five-pound sage grouse who got up and flew over the horizon after being knocked to the ground by peregrines; of falconers who rented airplanes and chased the fading radio bleeps of their gyrs two hundred miles; of falconers who backpacked into the Missouri Breaks country with a hawk and a dog and no food, to live off whatever they'd catch, who spent months in Plains Indian tepees with sage grouse and sharptails hanging from the meat pole, swaying in the endless wind. I heard repeated tales of professionals who gave up productive lives and moved their families to eastern Montana and northern Wyoming just to be near prairie grouse with their falcons.

All the stories were true, as I found out when I finally moved West myself. But it took me a while to see real grouse flights. As I wrote in 1984: "The grouse hawkers avoid publicity to the point of avoiding (nongrouse) falconers. Like all falconers they are basically self-made, having worked up to their precious gyrs through years of more common hawks; like all self-made men, they want others to pay their dues."

But finally Colonel Carnie invited me, with my late partner, Betsy Huntington, to Grouse Camp on the Llanos Estacados of New Mexico, and began a new chapter in my life. I still have Betsy's notes on that trip. They begin: "Arrive after 6½ hour drive. Stop at general store for directions (sealed) to Kent Carnie's grouse camp. Take left hand section road south of store; drive 9½ miles past pasture and grain fields. Road sandy, bordered from time to time with tumbled-down shacks from dustbowl days. Take indicated right hand turn and see metallic shining object that turns out to be Airstream trailer parked by deserted house, windmill, and two stock tanks. Cottontails abundant. Silence except for turn of windmill and rhythmic thump of pump. Nothing interrupts horizon. *Nothing.*"

If there is a more congenial host than Kent Carnie in the West or in the world, I'd love to meet him. Kansas born, Kent went from a degree in wildlife biology at UCLA to Army language school (in Arabic and Farsi) and then on to a career as an intelligence officer in the Near East that resembles that of a Kipling or Buchan hero, one of those legendary players of the "great game." Falconry is still a serious business in the Islamic countries, and Kent's interests brought him into repeated contact with the wealthy and powerful there. He managed to combine his pleasure with continued scientific work, trapping and banding falcons in places like the northern frontier of Iran, where few Westerners have ever been allowed.

He took his leaves in Scotland, hawking red grouse, where he met the aging legends of falconry and saw the best falcons of their time. And then retired at fifty, to return to his native Plains with plenty of time and ideas.

(Lest Kent sound like some latter-day incarnation of an English colonial, let me hasten to add that when I first met him he was wearing a T-shirt, shorts, and flip-flops, with his hybrid on one hand and a beer in the other, and that his taste in music ranges from Mozart and the Santa Fe Opera—he holds a season ticket—to Willie Nelson. And that at that time his hair was longer than mine. He more resembles a slightly westernized, authoritative English professor than anybody's stereotype of a military man. But, however necessarily, I digress.)

He was surprised to see us so early—twelve-fifteen, as we had left well before dawn—and offered us beer and cheese and music and stories. We were beginning to wonder if we were ever going to do anything but eat and drink when he suddenly checked his watch and said, "Well, it's *time*." And turned, instantly, from mild-mannered Dr. Carnie into a whole new fire-breathing personality that we might call Mr.—or Colonel—Falconer. In what seemed like seconds he had bundled us into the cab of his pickup truck and we were running down a dirt road at approximately seventy. "We've *got* to get there before four." Well, okay, though I had never seen falconry carried on with such precision.

Both the animal passengers seemed to take all this calmly. Muffin, an ancient Brittany, climbed into my lap, pressed her muzzle to the crack in the window, and drank air. On the backseat behind our head perched Blue Bell, a second-season peregrine hybrid that Betsy would later describe with only a little hyperbole as being "as big as a springer spaniel." She had big warm brown eyes, a back of darkest slate blue, and a black head marked like a hangman's hood. Her feet were as large as a small child's hands. As Kent cursed and spun the wheel and checked his watch she swayed and lowered her head to peer mildly through the windshield, as composed as a pet-store parrot.

Finally we pulled up at the edge of a mile-square field. Kent checked his watch for the thirteenth time and said, "I *think* we've made it. Look out over that way." He was pointing at the sky, which didn't make sense to me. However many times I had been told that prairie grouse were *different,* I still thought of them as chickenlike, earthy, grounded birds. And Kent's finger was indicating a point way above the horizon.

"There!" I squinted at the horizon and suddenly a line of movement, a crawl of dots, a wisp of blowing smoke came into focus. Above the ruled horizontal line between the dimming sky and the dirt was a flock of hundreds of birds, and they were coming our way.

I had never seen so many dry-land gamebirds; the flock was more like one of those clouds of blackbirds that move over farm fields and marshes like some many-eyed superorganism. Nor had I ever seen grouse in the sky. But I had little time to wonder. In about as long as it has taken for me to write these words they swung right, then left, and flopped into the field with set wings curved just below the horizontal. In a moment nothing was to be seen but a couple of round dark heads sticking up from the stubble glowing golden in the sunset; then they disappeared, too.

"*Mark those birds,*" commanded Kent. He clipped on Blue Bell's transmitter and climbed out. Falconers, real ones anyway, do not throw off their birds; they stand and let them choose their own moment for flight. Blue Bell knew her business. She ruffled her feathers, shook them down, lifted her tail to deposit a blob of white droppings, leaped into the air, and accelerated upwind as though she were equipped with jet engines.

As a good falcon will, she ignored the hidden grouse, but instead powered up into the sky in quick circles. In moments she leveled out, a black swallow's silhouette hundreds of feet above us, "waiting on" like a kite.

Now Kent *really* got excited. He snapped a lead on Muffin, patted his voluminous pockets for lures and receivers and such, then vaulted from the truck, motioning for us to follow. "Dammit, dammit, dammit, where are they?" he half whispered as he took off in a modified run toward the chickens' last point of visibility. Betsy later wrote: "He moves with extreme rapidity, looking oddly feminine from rear owing to his wearing a hip-length vest containing hawk furniture in the side pockets. Give him an odd sway as he walks swiftly through the fine dusty soil."

But again, we had little time to laugh. I had enough experience to know that no one is swift enough to watch both the hawk and the quarry, so I looked up toward Blue Bell just as the field erupted with hundreds of grouse. For a moment it seemed as though the entire surface of the field had lifted around me in my peripheral vision; wings thundered, and fifty separate voices called fearfully. But I kept my eyes on the falcon, who hovered, then fell, head forward, straight at the ground. For a moment she beat her wings, accelerating even faster than gravity's pull. Then she tucked them in to become an inverted heart shape shooting toward the prairie. I could hear the scream of stressed air whistling through her bells, rising high as she fell. As she neared the flock, she made an impossible right-angled turn parallel to the ground—I lost her for a second—and smashed past a grouse, tearing off a train of feathers that floated, suspended in the air. If I had been hit by that strike I'm sure I would have been stunned. But the grouse staggered in his flight, then recovered and pulled for the horizon. The hawk turned over fifty feet above him, fell again, missed, and headed after him. In a few seconds more all the birds were just beating notes on the darkening eastern horizon, then, quickly, invisible.

Incredibly, Kent seemed calm, much calmer than a moment before, as though the flight had purged him. "I *think*," he said, in a professorial mode, "that she got him. There's an old homestead just past this field, a mile over. She killed one there the day before yesterday. They head for the trees, for shelter." He swung his directional antenna toward the homestead and, after a moment, got a steady signal, rather than the fluctuating one that would indicate a flying bird. "See?"

It took fifteen minutes more to navigate the two sides of the section square to the abandoned house. It was dark enough for headlights. But when we entered the yard through the creaking gate, we saw Blue Bell perched calmly on the grouse's open breast, a single feather in her bill, two feet from the fence. She stepped sweetly to Kent's gloved fist as he murmured endearments, and I picked up my first prairie grouse.

■

To a falconer *grouse* does not mean that traditional shotgunner's favorite, the woodland ruffed grouse, but the much-less-celebrated bird of treeless country. Depending on how you view the matter taxonomically there are three or four species of prairie grouse: the sage grouse, the sharptail, and the two races of prairie chicken or pinnated grouse, greater and lesser. All share certain characteristics. Ruffed grouse seldom range more than a mile in a lifetime, and will rarely fly any farther than they have to to evade a predator. Prairie grouse seem sometimes to spend as much time in the sky as on the ground; they will fly over the horizon, and some gyrfalcon–sage grouse chases have gone ten miles. And all have had a more difficult time with humans than the ruffed, a noble creature that nevertheless still inhabits the Boston suburb where I grew up. They are *wild*.

The largest, wildest, and least adaptable of them is the great sage grouse, the largest grouse in North America and the second largest in the world; males can weigh up to seven pounds. Sage grouse live in, live on, and smell like sage; if it is destroyed, they vanish. Some shotgun hunters scorn them as easy targets, but the hardest-core grouse hawkers of all celebrate them as the ultimate gamebird. Many peregrines simply can't handle them; small birds have been killed by their voluntary midair collisions with such immovable objects. Add to this the biggest, wildest, and most remote ranges, where even ranches are fifty miles apart, winter temperatures are forty below zero, and the constant deadly presence of the aerial rulers of the sage country—golden eagles, which will as happily kill and eat a falcon as they will steal her sage grouse—and you know why some falconers treasure this bird.

The most naturally adaptable of the prairie grouse is the sharptail. It is found from Alaska to Manitoba and south to Wyoming; unlike its cousins, it is tolerant of trees. It is, to quote Jim Weaver, "harder and slicker" than the other birds—its feathers are "almost like scales." It may be the most difficult aerial evader of the three; Wyoming falconer Pete Widener has taken movies of sharptails escaping his gyr, which, when slowed down, reveal the grouse doing complete barrel rolls to dodge from beneath the hawk. And its country, if more inhabited than that of the sage, is at least as cold.

But my favorite, the species that William Least-Heat Moon calls the Plains' "signature bird" itself, is the pinnated grouse of the longgrass prairie, and its "lesser" relative of the southern High Plains. The lesser is arguably the prettiest, with its head plumes and yellow eye combs and distinct barring. It lives in the remnant oceanic high grasslands of the Comancheria, one of the finest and least-celebrated wild lands left to us. Its mating dance is truly amazing, an almost-human strut and bow and display that makes you think you might be seeing reincarnated ghosts of the old inhabitants.

Prairie chickens apparently boomed as the sodbusters came in, then nearly disappeared. (A related eastern bird, the heath hen, is extinct.) Now they hang on in rather limited numbers. They are a species of ecotones, surviving on the moving edge of cultivation and shinnery oak, of sandhills and milo fields. Jim Weaver believes they were migratory, or rather nomadic; that they followed the buffalo. Least-Heat Moon says it well: "The bird thrives on moderate grazing and fire only every few years: too much of either can do it in, as can too much cultivated land; in other words, this signal bird, so easy to recognize and to anthropomorphize, is an excellent load-indicator, a sign of how much the grass country can bear, an emblem of a diverse and balanced prairie, the requirements of bird aligning with those of men."

■

In the sixties it seemed like the peregrine was a miner's canary, indicating the contamination of the environment by its response to DDT. The species is still one of the most widespread in the world, found on all continents but Antarctica and all oceanic islands but the most remote. But those populations most exposed to man, the ones in Europe and North America, were disappearing, victims of DDT-induced eggshell thinning. By 1968 they had vanished as a breeding species in the eastern half of the United States.

Perhaps, if such a thing could have happened in medival times, kings and nobles would have rallied to the bird's cause; certainly they valued the peregrine, restricting its use to those of noble birth. In the twentieth century, the peregrine and its salvation became the holy cause of a little band of old-fashioned hands-on hunter-naturalists, falconers to a man (and, later, woman). Tom Cade, a professor at the Cornell Laboratory of Ornithology, founded the Peregrine Fund in 1969 to set up a facility to breed falcons there. Many doubted that it could be done. But with seed stock from falconers, he proved them wrong. Then the doubters claimed that the released birds would never hunt for themselves. Using "hacking," a falconer's technique for teaching captive-raised babies to hunt, he proved them wrong again.

He hired Jim Weaver in 1971, to supervise the program. Weaver is an original. Born in Illinois, he ran away from home in the fifties to work as a bird bander for Frances and Frederick Hamerstrom, grand eccentrics and ornithological legends who had studied under Aldo Leopold and made a life's work of the greater prairie chicken. Later he had earned a degree in wildlife biology, but was better known as a daring and committed falconer. Cade hired him at ten thousand dollars a year as a technical associate — you had to have a Ph.D. to be a research associate. For the next eighteen years Weaver would work a schedule that would have killed a less driven man, supervising the "hawk barn" and hack sites that ranged from Yellowstone to New York City, flying his own plane from site to site. He spent part of each summer kayaking wilderness rivers in Greenland, censusing peregrines, climbing cliffs, and banding young. Later he began commuting to Zimbabwe, where he became involved in evaluation and protecting the raptors of the Zambezi River.

Meanwhile, other falconers, including Dan O'Brien and I, became hack-site attendants, spending our summers guarding the babies' transformation into predatory adults. The result, nearly twenty years later, is one of the few great recent success stories in conservation: The peregrine is once again a common sight on the cliffs, on the coasts, and even in the cities of the West. And the species owes it all to this quixotic band.

■

"BLM land, good water, fantastic scenery—and, best of all, no people."
—Jim Weaver

Weaver wrote those words years ago but since then even he, the fiercest of us all, has mellowed a bit. Forty-degree-below-zero nights can seem colder when you are pushing fifty with a metal pin in your leg; besides, Jim now has a four-year-old son, and he says, not entirely joking, "It's hard to be a legend when you find a pacifier in your hawking bag."

Yet somehow a lot of us still find time to gather south of Portales at the end of winter. Once, Grouse Camp meant just that: a series of nomads' tents and trailers spread out from Montana to Texas. Now, more and more, it means the rendezvous on the southern Plains where we all come together at season's end. It is a time and place for reminiscence, for storytelling and memories; and, at the end of each day, a flight. Falconers are not really misanthropes—we just need space. And habitat, and the company of our kind.

As do the grouse. These days the attention of the Grouse Camp crew has focused on prey, on habitat; on, could we say, home? Cade is in Idaho, working for the Peregrine Fund's new World Center for Birds of Prey. Its latest focus, now that the peregrine is moving out of danger, is on tropical raptors, endangered in the rain forest. Dan O'Brien is ranching in South Dakota and worried about the prairie. Idaho's Charles Schwartz, formerly the falcon-breeding adviser to the Sheikh of Bahrain, has built a house at his own grouse camp, on the edge of one of the greatest pieces of roadless sage desert left. On a recent trip I stood beside him on a hill overlooking its blue-green expanse as he expounded on threats to its integrity from grazing and, more ominously, sage-busting farming. Charles is not known for diplomacy: He gestured over the plain, saying, "You're a writer; you've got to help us *do* something about this!"

And Jim Weaver, home at least for the moment from his travels, has bought and built on a piece of land that he has hunted for almost twenty years, where he hopes to pioneer a kind of stewardship that has a place for both humans and prairie chickens. He knows that you can't tell people what to do; you've got to show them. He hopes, when all his plans are working, to have water points every quarter section; a few cattle, tame emus, some row crops and strip plantings; original prairie grasses, or as close to original as can be reconstructed; deer, coyotes, wild raptors, songbirds, beetles, bobwhite quail, and, of course, as many lesser prairie chickens as possible.

Which is why, this year, we won't be hawking grouse at all. Last evening, as I raced the setting sun down the last few miles of dirt road to Weaver's house, I saw the familiar silhouettes dropping into the mile east of the homestead; a little flock, maybe twenty birds. Jim was delighted. "That's more than I've seen there all year. Three years of drought have brought the numbers way down. Tomorrow we can fly Seeker—but we'll just have to chase quail or doves. It's a shame, but there just aren't enough to kill any."

In the morning I wake to the sweet whistles of bobwhite quail and the creak of blackbirds. Stepping out of O'Brien's adobe "cabin," mine for the weekend since Dan is occupied up north, my spaniel Bart and I bump three cottontails before I reach the outhouse. A redtail launches from the corner post of the horse corral. When I leave the outhouse, movement on the horizon catches my eye and I watch three wary deer file into the oak-covered sandhills to the west. The Plains may be dry, but they're a bountiful "desert."

We drive all day down Jim's dirt roads, inspecting tanks and taking census. We see a dozen raptors. (He is doing banding studies of nesting Swainson's hawks and barn owls, as well as banding migrant redtails, harriers, and prairie falcons.) We count deer tracks and flush quail. Jim shows me nests of Chihuahuan ravens, Swainson's hawks, and scissor-tailed flycatchers in the infrequent trees. We fish dead rats out of watering troughs, pat the emus ("dinosaurs," says Jim), and discuss P-Fund projects in Central America and Zimbabwe. Finally, when the sun is its own height above the horizon, it's time to fly the hawk.

Seeker is a male gyrfalcon-peregrine of fourteen years, old, wise, and calm. His feathers are a deep slate blue, with hints of plum on his breast. He sits unruffled on Jim's fist as I let out the dogs and Jim slips his hood on, for discipline's sake.

Things immediately get silly. There are five dogs: Dan, an ancient deaf setter; a new and talented but high-strung female pointer who tends to head for the horizon; a serious German shorthaired pointer, also female; my male spaniel Bart, eight years old and as serious as a springer ever gets; and the ultimate goof, Jim's year-old male saluki, Lateef, whose greatest joy is to course and harass the bird dogs.

As we fan out on the prairie the pointer heads for the horizon, followed by Lateef and, hopelessly behind, Dan. Bart and the shorthair attempt to imitate the pattern of windshield wipers just ahead of us.

Suddenly the pointer crouches, tail flagging, moves forward left a foot, right the same, and freezes. I signal to Bart to "hup," spaniel for "sit." Jim unhoods Seeker, who climbs in rapid circles.

But before he reaches a pitch of more than a hundred feet, two things happen. The three distant dogs come racing back just as one of Jim's homing pigeons, mistakenly left out when we locked up, comes into sight over the trees. The hawk checks at the pigeon just as the dogs gallop up. The quail, seeing its opportunity, flushes and races for the sandhills, followed by all but the shorthair and Bart.

Jim sighs. After a moment the falcon returns and begins to circle low over our heads; most falcons, even gyrs, find tailchasing pigeons to be a hopeless exercise. Jim swings the lure, the leather bird-shaped object used to call in a falcon, and lets it fall. Seeker shoots in with a hiss of primaries and strikes it, hard.

As the bird feeds, the sun sets, and the dogs pant, Jim grins at me. "You're not going to write about *this* flight, are you?"

"I have an obligation to the truth." I'm grinning, too, of course.

He sighs again. *"Falconry on the High Plains: The Romance."*

Well, yes.

Unpublished (1992)

PART III

Sport

A Canvas, Ever
Changing

Hunter safety courses, hook and bullet magazines, even some well-meaning and serious books, seem to take the subject of how we behave in the field as a fixed subject, a collection of rules. To me the concept has always seemed more elusive. In our society, still enamored of the old Vince Lombardi "winning is the *only* thing" standard, we might have to uncouple our understanding of field sports from ball games and such to truly understand them, and to come to a concept of honor that does justice to the animals that we hunt and kill.

The underlying principle of honor in the field is *honor*. We must *honor* the animals that we pursue; otherwise, we shouldn't be killing them. The idea of honor to me stretches from closed seasons to learning cookery that pleasess. I've always been uneasy with hunters and fishers who give away all their meat, although grateful for the generosity. Hunting is a play about life and death and the transfer of energy, but if we stray too far from eating, I question the seriousness of our play.

Hunting ethics go a lot farther than laws and rules, which determine a minimum or arbitrary set of lines. They involve a lifelong commitment to keeping your eyes open. You can teach a child the rules of gun safety, or how to cast, by rote and repetition. Ethics involve example over a long period, talk, and, above all, thought.

I am, say, nine years old. I know my father hunts, and I have eaten venison. I love to handle the black ducks he brings home, admiring the metallic blue speculum edged in blue and black on each wing, trying frustratedly to reproduce the color with my colored pencils.

We keep homing pigeons. My father is a fiercely competitive, driven man, given to long silences, brooding, occasional explosions. He does not take me hunting yet; looking back, I think he knows his own impatience, and fears it. But he does let me take care of and handle our racers. He makes all the decisions about mating, training, culling, life, and death. Still, I allow myself favorites and enjoy watching them move and behave and strut in the sun. It's like having a great walk-in aquarium.

I especially like to watch them fly, in endless sweeping circles around our backyard, beating upwind, sliding down, climbing until they look like vibrating specks, shooting by just over the roof, where I can hear the sibilant hiss of a hundred wings.

I like "splashed" birds, piebald magpie-patterned pigeons with vivid mixes of black or blue and white. My father doesn't. I don't know why until one windy day, as I watch the birds circle, a gray-and-white hawk rips through the flock like an artillery shell, leaving a trail of floating feathers, and turns to grab the wounded pigeon, a splash, and drags it down on the other side of the trees. I run in and scream for my father, who comes out and stares at the tree line, scratching his head. The flock is now almost out of sight in the sky, bunched as tight as starlings. I'm sure I know where the hawk is. "Can you shoot it?"

My father shakes his head. I think back now and imagine that I can see his frustration; he never was one to explain much. "No. We don't shoot hawks." I wait for an explanation, but he just shakes his head again. "Let me know when the birds come down."

"But it's my *splash*, the young one." I don't dare say more; clearly, he isn't pleasured by the loss, but he is also—I understand now—a member of the Massachusetts Audubon Society.

"That's why I don't like them. Hawks go after white. And we *don't shoot hawks.*" He turns and goes in. Clearly, the matter is finished.

But it does start me thinking, and reading, about hawks. Looking back, though he thought it was a "duck hawk," a peregrine, I believe it was a male goshawk. One sits in my yard right now.

■

At seventeen I found a mentor, Ralph. He was a paper mill worker and a master falconer. A chain-smoker, a fly fisherman, a surf caster of great expertise, a wingshooter with one old gun (a cut-down Browning humpback auto with a silver-gray finish). A mechanic, a bowhunter, a man who figured out how to make a crossbow out of a leaf spring from an old truck chassis.

He would not necessarily be a hero to the textbook set. I know that one winter, laid off from the mill, he—without bad conscience—killed two deer with his crossbow, to feed his family. (Need I say that the deer herd in coastal New England is . . . not endangered?) But he was a gentleman hunter-gatherer with respect and reverence, better than a mere "sportsman," though he was that, too. He had a pair of wild goshawks who would follow him around and take pigeons from his hands; he had movies. He had an old redtail, a trained bird, who stayed loose for a year and a half, but who would come when he called.

What he taught me—no small lesson—was to be polite to animals. He was polite and reverent to *all* animals, not just "his." He would still wince at how noisy I am on a stream bank; he could stalk individual trout like a cat.

But mostly he was polite to hawks. One day he was walking down the railroad tracks between two stretches of pheasant cover with a young male goshawk on his fist. The bird, inadequately named "Spooky," was a savage-tempered imprint with the good habit of chasing anything that moved. But he would bounce off your head like an ill-tempered human if he missed his strike, or, sometimes, for no reason at all. You wanted to know where he was, because if you lost track of him he would knock your hat off or plow furrows in your scalp.

Ralph saw something at the tree line and raised his bare hand to point. Spooky didn't hesitate; he slammed out with one foot and locked onto the hand, without relinquishing his hold on the glove, effectively handcuffing Ralph with a fistful of needles, pressed in with enough force to drive to the bone.

It took Ralph more than a few seconds to get my attention, because he would not yell around hawks except to call them in. He was trying to call me in a whisper, but I didn't realize that anything was wrong until I looked back and saw him hunched over the bird in what looked like an attitude of prayer. When I saw how white his face was, I began to jog toward him. He was whispering again.

"What?"

"*Slow down.*" Still in a whisper. As I approached I could see the problem.

"What can I do?"

"Nothing. Just be ready to take him up when he lets go. I need to bandage this."

We waited ten minutes by my watch, while blood ran down Ralph's arm, until the goggle-eyed hawk finally let go and settled his ruffled feathers. I took him, with some trepidation, while Ralph improvised a bandage. He just shook his head and laughed, maybe a little hollowly: "Serves me right for waving my hand around where he could grab it." He looked me in the eye. "Never try to pry a hawk off yourself. Even if you can do it, she'll hate you for a week."

■

Not long after that incident I shot a grouse that came tumbling down in a flurry of feathers and landed with a thump in some open leaf litter. Fifteen minutes later, I still couldn't find it.

I had not been grouse hunting long. My father had tried to "teach" me, but his talents did not lie in teaching. He would let me carry a .410 and make one shot; if I missed, as I always did, he would not let me shoot again. I had been on my own since I was seventeen, and now possessed a 20-bore side-by-side Browning. I was not so good a shot that I didn't greedily devour every bird I hit, with all my senses. So I cannot say that it was—at first—any concept of "honor" that had me looking so hard for that lost bird; it was more a kind of loss of a possible, if temporary, possession.

But it began to bother me. I kept thinking that, if it were dead, it wouldn't be so damn hard to find. It must be wounded, and hiding. I have always been imaginative, perhaps a little too imaginative, I thought then, to be a hunter. (Now I think I was not imaginative enough. Another story. . . .) I had been raised on Seton and such tales of dying animals. I began to worry about the bird. I got down on my hands and knees and began to comb through the leaves.

I searched from about three in the afternoon until dark—five-thirty? I poked my hand into logs, kicked brushpiles, crawled along with my nose six inches from the ground. I never found the bird.

The next day I wrote a letter to the outdoor columnist of the *Boston Globe*, a wonderful writer who I knew wasn't too many years older than I, asking him how I, a member of the baby-boom generation estranged from my honorable but impossible father, could learn how to hunt birds "in the proper tradition." His answer, a column, earned him the status of mentor in my memory, although we only met for the first time twenty-some years later. The title of the column was "Find Yourself a Gentleman with a Dog."

■

I should have; I didn't. Long haired, rebellious, shy, I found myself unable to ask. But I did find myself a dog, my first springer: Spud, named without irony after the first hunting dog I had ever known, a springer who belonged to my father's hunting partner when I was a toddler.

Spud was no perfect dog; he wasn't even of pure field stock. He was huge and sometimes surly, with an ominous streak of the "springer rage syndrome" peculiar to show-strain males. But he loved birds, and usually me, and—without reservation—my late partner, Betsy Huntington.

Who, though she hadn't been a hunter—she was raised by one— began to teach me other facets of honor in the field.

First, honor your dog, and not just in the field, for everything connects to everything. Spud, was, as I said, moody, as moody as my father—or me. One night after a hard sleety day in the field he approached the bed growling for no reason I could see. Annoyed, I told him to go lie down. He ignored me and growled louder. Suddenly furious myself, I threw my paperback in his face. Betsy got up, took the dog by the collar, and led him to his bed in the corner, where she remained a moment, calming him. She returned to bed, gave me a long icy look, and said, "Do not *ever* punish a dog the way your father punished you."

I still wince at the words, the only harsh ones I can remember that she ever spoke to me. I never again punished a dog in such a way.

She had her own subtle ideas of honor toward the prey as well. Back in those days we used to course various quarry with greyhounds. When we were alone we only ran jackrabbits, but our coursing mentor, Floyd Mansell, also chased coyotes. I have never been entirely comfortable killing coyotes and, after Betsy's death, gave it up. But I suspect there's a bit of sentimentality in my refusal, and I wonder if her own attitude was not more respectful. After listening to my endless examinations of conscience, she wrote to a friend: "We find ourselves ambivalent about the coyote's death, particularly Steve, who rather identifies with predators. I don't know 'bout that. If either of us were as good predators as your run-of-the-mill coyote, I might feel greater kinship. As it is, I sort of tip my eyebrow at him if I see him (not having a suitable hat or sex for tipping that, and it not being my nature to curtsy without a suitable skirt) and feel, well, if he loses, he loses, just like you or me."

■

Dogs will always present you with problems, conundrums, solutions. What do you do when your eager saluki suddenly busts up a covey of quail while searching for hares, leaps, snatches one out of the air, and brings it to your hand? (The day is three weeks before quail season opens up.) Berate him, hit him with the bird, praise him? "Let it lie," behind, in the field? Take it home and put it in the freezer?

What about when your spaniel, while you are hunting woodcocks, keeps on sneaking onto the adjacent private estate to bring back planted pheasants — many of which seem to have been shot and left?

What about *believing* dogs? Old Spud, no genius, once persisted in hanging back and refusing to go on in dense cover. Nowadays I would consider that I had made a shot, and that he might have something to tell me. "Nowadays," of course, is made up of experiences like that time when, impatient, I pushed on, only to have Spud return twenty minutes later with a dead woodcock that he brought to my hand.

(A good dog, of course, is more conscientious about such things than even the most earnest human. Ten years later Bart, my present spaniel, hung back after a shot, then delivered to me an *extremely* dead woodcock. From its state of decay — despite frosty weather — I suspect it had been there at least a week. What do you do then? Throw it away? Put the stinking thing in your pocket?)

Listen to your dogs.

■

If you are a reader there are of course other teachers, living and dead. Two excellent English fly-fishing books made me question the dogma of "purist" catch-and-release, and put me at odds with some of the contemporaries I respect most. A. Luce, an Irish philosopher, wrote a book called *Fishing and Thinking* in 1959; Bryn Hammond, a much younger man, wrote *Halcyon Days* in 1992. Luce's viewpoint was almost theological; you *had* to kill and eat your fish, because "to hook trout and put them back into the water, unless they are too small to keep and quite uninjured, is to inflict pain, however small the amount, unnecessarily, and it therefore comes under the definition of cruelty. . . . It involves the infliction of pain without the hunter's justification for doing so." Bryn Hammond is much more moderate, and closer to the opinions I have formed. He believes in catch-and-release, but worries that it will become another dogma. "Catch and release is not merely an art of fly fishing, not necessarily learned or suitable for some fishermen, but it is one that should be used only on waters where it makes real sense and not simply imagined sense. Where and when it is practised, it should always be for the sake of the trout, not for the sake of the angler. If any benefits accrue from its employment then they are due to the fish alone. If not, then it becomes an act of selfishness."

Unexceptionable? I would think so. But I have felt a certain distance from some catch-and-release purist friends since I published my agreement with these positions. I stand by my bottom line, which is: We must fish, hunt, *think*, read, debate, read, think. . . .

Charles Schwartz, a student of mine in writing but not in falconry—he is and always will be a mentor in that—challenged me with a story. As I commented, wrote in the margins, helped him shape the words, the words were shaping me. His thesis? In hawking, in sport, in life, don't hold on so hard. But he is too good a writer to "tell." His story is of a young falconer with a merlin, a tiny songbird hawk of the

High Plains. He weighs her down with bells, calls her when she strays, and catches nothing; she simply perches on fence posts, refuses to chase. Eventually an old master shows him, without comment. Takes the bells off his bird, feeds it up to high condition, lets it go. The young man tries the same, despite his fears, and sees a fabulous flight. The story works. What Charlie doesn't know is that I now let my birds fly, and don't call them back when they approach the horizon.

There are friends you meet after you have read them, after your practice in the field (or at your desk) has been changed by them. I am privileged to cite many—John Barsness, Charley Waterman, Nick Lyons, Tom McGuane, to name a few almost at random. But I am now thinking of a near neighbor in Montana, Datus Proper. I first read his book on fishing, then his books on pheasants and Portugal, all the time keeping up a light-hearted correspondence with him from New Mexico. ("This postcard has a picture of *water.* Do you remember *water?*") When I began spending half my time in Montana we started to hunt together. Our styles fit together smoothly, except for the fact that he has legs twice as long as mine, and so can walk over fences I have to climb. We enjoy each other's company.

But I never thought of him as another mentor until, seduced by the endless Plains, I began to think of getting a pointer. Of course, I didn't want just *any* pointer. Despite having had to learn the lesson again and again, with tackle and guns (and clothes and books and stereos and . . .), I wanted the "best," best being inevitably the most prestigious, something that would (I dared not admit) impress my friends. I wanted an English pointer or setter that would work the horizon, freeze to point with an almost-audible snap. Since Datus had written *Pheasants of the Mind,* a book that included a chapter with the wonderful title "A Pointer of the Veronese School," I kept bugging him. What breed, what breeder, what training? What sex, strain, size? What color? How much should I pay?

It's easy enough for anyone, even someone who knows better, to substitute snobbishness for real standards, custom for the harder dictates of honor. It does not matter if you shoot your capercaillie sitting, as the Austrians do, or in a drive like the Scots. It doesn't matter what shotgun you shoot, whether it's a double or a pump. (Jack O'Connor was once asked whether a double was "the gentleman's gun." He replied that it was scarcely the only criterion.) Wealthy Americans often forget this. We won't even talk about the English who shoot driven game. I've been guilty, even though I know better. I used to think that it showed enough respect to "shoot a pretty bird with a pretty gun." It doesn't. I still shoot an obscure English double—I hit better with its lightweight grace after I have walked a long way—but I also shoot an old pump, *because I kill more cleanly with it than with most other 12s.*

In the same way, it is not more "sporting" to use line so light that it wears fish out. (Read the Scottish naturalist and salmon expert Hugh Falkus on this one.) Nor to use a rifle caliber too light to do the job. Beware of 2-weight rods, .243s, .410s, and 28s in the hands of wealthy nonexperts.

And having figured all this out, I was still applying aesthetic snobbery to dogs.

Datus is a gentleman with two dogs, both shorthairs, a scholar by temperament, a man with opinions. What he is not is didactic; he doesn't tell you what to do any more than mentors, dogs, the best books. He would say things like, "I'm not a breed man. It's the dog." He would tell me stories about Huck, his older (and wonderful) dog. He gave me an essay to read—one that was to be added to a new edition of his pheasant book—"for editorial comment." He'd tell me about a field-trial pointer he once owned, who could point but not think.

Finally my thick skull absorbed his points. I wanted a dog that was a natural, and could think. Style was less important. I wanted a dog that could trail if it was necessary, which might be a fault in a field-trial dog. Breed was unimportant, strain and intelligence were everything. To quote from his essay: "Discipline and judgment are opposite qualities. Of the two, discipline is the safer choice because it requires not thinking; judgment is a learning process."

Hunting and thinking, to paraphrase Luce. (Datus—coincidentally?—wrote an intro for the latest edition of his book.) Listen.

■

And if you can teach someone—son, daughter, buddy, the other half of your couple, reader, protegé, or protegée—teach them to listen, not just to what you say, but also to what the wind and the animals and the dead hunters say. And teach them to keep listening, keep thinking, and keep formulating their ideas.

My stepson, Jackson, is nineteen. He has long since passed his hunter safety course and has killed three deer. Last year he bought a custom longbow from a local maker. I am pleased to see that he does not yet use it in the field, because, he candidly admits, "I'm not good enough yet."

These are the things I watch. He now goes to a local informal shotgun course to shoot with his mother. He handles my proud touchy goshawk, Sara, with grace and gentleness; she likes him, and not too many goshawks accept more than one servant. He listens to her—she has taught him to move slowly, to keep his bird hand high and his other hand low. She'll sometimes turn her sickle-billed head upside down to greet him. I think he'll be a hunter, a real one, which means he will show honor in the field.

■

Hunting ethics is not a set of rules, not a mere discipline. To me it's ever changing, not from one thing to another but more like a palimpsest, a painting, becoming ever clearer as we work the canvas with new overlays and strokes; a canvas, ever-changing, sometimes muddy; finally, if you work at it enough, clearer.

Comissioned for an anthology that was never published (1996)

Home Again

You *can't* go home again. And yet, and yet . . . for seven years in the Southwest I had dreamed of old grouse and woodcock coverts. Though bird numbers ebbed and flowed, those particular spots in southeastern Massachusetts seemed suspended in time.

There were two main concentrations of birds. One was more a series than a single covert, a chain of old fields studded with juniper and containing clumps of thorns and wild roses the size of small houses, strung out along the railroad track. Though the forest encroached subtly on the edges, some lack of fertility in the pasture had kept it at bay for twenty years. The other was more stable and therefore more confusing. It was a real classic New England tangle of bayberries and crab apples, crossed by a power-line cut, walled in by eighty-foot white pines. Though close behind a line of old houses, it was the most consistently productive spot for grouse I have ever known. Its neighbors seemed more than tolerant, waving as you entered or left, stopping to inquire after an old dog or a new gun.

I try not to romanticize these things. Nostalgia is the curse of bird-hunting writing, perhaps even more of upland-hunting writing. There is something about the eternal cold so close below the surface of fall's transient glory that heightens the hunter's awareness of mortality and time passing. Add in the necessary deaths of birds and, maybe, the mismatched life span of man and dog, and it becomes tempting to evoke the easy sigh, the fleeting tear. I have been scornful of others doing so in the past, and I won't yield. Still, when the random forces that play on our lives brought me reluctantly back to New England for a season, I knew there were two pleasures available: grouse and woodcocks. And I was sure that my best opportunities would flush from the coverts of my childhood.

My animals and books, gear and possessions, all my beloved and irritating encumbrances, were stashed in at least ten places, from Silver City, New Mexico (a saluki), to Oklahoma City (a double 4-bore muzzleloader) to Amherst and Newton and Easton, Massachusetts. My station wagon was in Magdalena with my pigeons. All I had in Maine were a basic kit of books, a hybrid falcon, two of my spaniels, and (of course) a couple of birdguns.

If you are an upland gunner, your season begins long before opening day. I was renting two rooms in an old farmhouse owned by a friend who was something of a sporting obsessive. Fanning shoots birds, goes to Quebec to hunt caribou, flies hawks, runs bird dogs, fishes for trout and salmon, and traps. He also teaches school and rebuilds houses, and rents out rooms to subsidize these various activities. Counting me, the farm was inhabited by four human hunters, three English setters, two springers, two hybrid falcons, two goshawks, two breeding pairs of prairie falcons, and a loft of pigeons. The guns housed there could have equipped a Third World country. The house stands on a dead-end road that empties into the yard of another friend, who also runs a setter. Two more setter breeders and another two falconers live within five minutes' drive. After the second week in August, any late afternoon would see at least one of those dogs quartering the field across the street in search of a planted pigeon, with two or three or four humans dancing attendance. The snaps of .22 blanks and shouts of "Whoa!" punctuated my writing afternoons, until I could no longer work and would cross the street to hold a leash or shoot a training pistol. Dinner was often delayed or, if the Scotch and bourbon flowed freely enough, ignored, as we talked about the past and coming seasons, waving our arms and taking imaginary shots in a cloud of cigar smoke.

Of my own dogs, the female, Sass, is an impossible if charming prima donna of vast intelligence, good nose, and no discipline. Kept as a brood female and pet, she never got any serious field training and has steadfastly resisted any latter-day attempts to cure the situation. Bart, the male, is good and always willing. Bart walks at heel, trembles with eagerness, flies off riverbanks to hit the river with a mighty splash. (A friend once remarked to a springer trainer that his dogs hit the water like Labs. The man was insulted: "It takes a *damn good* Lab to hit the water like a springer.") Bart had some second-rate professional training that seemed to have left him with the impression that you use eyes first, then ears, then-and-only-then the nose to find birds, though his nose works perfectly well when he is off duty. Running open-country quail had done nothing to correct this trait. I was hoping that dense cover and smelly close-holding woodcocks would.

I took Bart to the open woodland along the Saco as September began to loosen leaves in the riverside thickets. The second time we took that walk we bumped a woodcock that whistled for the nearest hole in the canopy. Bart looked apologetic—I had criticized his interest in songbirds out West—then slightly confused as I sang his praises: "Good Bart, found the *bird. Good* Bart." A week of this and he no longer looked back and rolled his eyes when a 'cock twittered up. Still, he showed more enthusiasm for the stocked pheasants in John's nearby estate, or even pigeons, be they planted in the farm field or grazing on the lawn. He was fetching the dummy with dispatch, churning after it like a paddlewheeler when I fired it into the river's current with the Retrieve-R-Trainer, and nearly losing his mind every time I picked up a gun. Despite his lukewarm enthusiasm for 'cocks—we had no grouse—I figured we were ready to roll.

But not on the river, not yet. My quarry was not just home birds, but some sense of old times. Opening day found me down in Massachusetts, where the season was delayed ten more days. For all the attractions of southern Maine, I knew that the past still tugged at me, that no New England season would be complete unless I started in Easton.

I hadn't parked by either covert in at least five years. The first, bigger one has its own parking lot, built for a restaurant that burned down twenty years ago. Always, at least since I was eleven, you had entered behind it and followed an overgrown road lined with wild grapes on the high ground, alders below, thorns everywhere, flushing grouse from every likely spot. When you reached the tracks there were three choices: the dense tangles along a little stream on the far side of the cow pasture; the overgrown fields across the tracks, where most birds would be feeding on crab apples and a woodcock was almost always a possibility; or, most productive and usually saved for last, the huge tangles of roses on the way out. I was full of anticipation and, yes, nostalgia. I had hunted these patches with many friends and dogs, including one of each no longer living.

But as soon as I stepped off the broken tar edge of the pavement, anticipation changed to something like dread. From the head of the old road all the way to the tracks, someone had bulldozed a straight raw dirt path. I had never seen the entire distance before, and it seemed pathetically short to an eye now accustomed to western vistas. Worse, the whole strip was full of collapsed green trash bags spilling garbage, bottles, and cans.

I cut off to the left and began to explore. Most of the thorn covert was intact. But though the dogs crossed back and forth within tight gun range, tunneling through thorns, tails flagging, nothing flushed. Then we were through it, looking at an area of incomprehensible devastation. An acre of trees had been felled and left, leaving an area almost impossible to cross with a gun and two dogs—a giant's pile of jackstraws. Despite the fact that in the suburbs wood was now going for about $120 a cord, it looked like it had been on the ground for at least a season.

We circled, seeing only more trash and beer cans. I led the way to the brook, *knowing* a grouse would buzz out of the grapevine tangle just where I had been caught a dozen times balanced above the stream, gun broken open, cursing. I would have welcomed it this time. Still, silence, no bird—*nada*.

On the way back I saw a bunch of young teenagers perched atop a huge glacial boulder. In the fifties I had spent more than one afternoon there myself. They nodded sullenly to my wave, even as I might have then. I was an adult intruder in their private world. Just before I reached the truck the dogs stopped hard, quivering, almost like pointers. I thought, "Bird!" Then Bart growled, and I noticed that their ruffs were bristling. Less than fifty feet away two deer stared at us. The wind was in our faces and, from the buck's lowered tail, it was obvious that they did not believe we were real. I gripped the dogs' collars and yelled, "Shoo!" Even then it took a moment before they moved off in their hesitant march step, still not spooked enough to run. In twenty years I had never seen a deer there, nor failed to raise a bird.

The second covert was even more unnerving. It looked unchanged from the truck. But as I stepped out to remove my gun from its sleeve and heel up the dogs, a tall man of my own age all but ran up from the nearest house. "Are you planning to *hunt?*" He gave "hunt" a peculiar emphasis, like, "Are you planning to *molest my children?*"

"Yes. Don't worry—I'm going in far enough that . . ."

"The hell you are. What kind of maniac are you? This is a residential area!"

"I've been hunting here for twenty years."

"Then it's about time you stopped. If you're not out of here in five minutes, I'm calling the cops. I'm counting. . . ."

He was looking at his watch, flushed with his heroism. Legality was likely on my side. But living in the Deep West for seven years had snapped my ability to deal with his attitude. It wasn't the kind of glorious combative *fun* it had been when I seemed to be the only human predator in Newton, Massachusetts. I slid my Darne back into its sleeve. It was time to go to Maine, if not the High Plains—some kind of home, with some of home's familiar comforts.

■

Saturday afternoon in Bar Mills, a golden day, almost too warm. At this point I was conscious that I was making a ritual out of the return, striving for a perfection that I knew down deep I had never attained back when. The whole thing had taken on so much importance that I was nervous. Even if everything else went well, I was afraid that the intensity of my desire would pull my shots off target. Every detail had to be perfect. Leave Sass home. She's too spooky and hard to control. Take the straight-gripped Darne, you shoot it better than the others. The right outfit: the battered birdshooters; field pants with suspenders, not the belt, the better to hold up the shells. Twelve shells, 20 bore, ⅞ ounce of 8s—too many for a three-bird limit, but better to be safe. Five in each pocket, two for the gun. The old L. L. Bean chamois shirt, the gray thirties-style fedora with the moth holes, once too elegant for a birdshooter's hat, but after seven years in New Mexico's weather just perfect.

To the kennel, where my hunting house pets must live in Maine. "Stay, Sass, *stay* dammit. Bart, you hup. *Sit.*" I put on his bell, which made him wriggle in ecstasy on his back. ("Sit *still*, you moron!") He knew what this all meant. Then around the fence and into the woods. ("Heel. Good boy. *Good.* Heel.") No cars needed here.

The path led steeply down to the river's floodplain. As I reached the flat I heard a voice from above. "Steve? Are you hunting?" It was Mark Black, another of the dog crowd, who had been running his young setter Ben across the street. He is a falconer who doesn't shoot. Most hawk trainers like a dog to have one or even two seasons of gun work before it is introduced to the extra demands of falconry, so Mark had been hoping to work his dog with the farm's shooters.

"I need to work Bart. Why don't you kennel up Ben and come on out? If I manage to shoot something over him, we'll come back and take out Ben."

"That's fair."

We worked one of those long loops. In known coverts, I'd rather save the best for last. Bart worked in the spaniel's patented windshield-wiper pattern, back and forth across our path. As we got down to the dead-flat, leaf-strewn, open-canopy forest toward the river, I wiggled my elbows to loosen up; raised the gun to a more perfect port arms; checked to see that my index was ready to work the Darne's peculiar safety. Suddenly Bart tensed and stopped. "Look at him!" said Mark. (Like most setter men, he believed deep down that all flushing dogs do is accidentally stir up game.) Bart's head was low, his tail whipping left and right.

"I know, I see. Bart, *git* 'em!" Private language. Bart started forward, wriggling all over, almost crawling, as a 'cock came up with an explosive series of whistles. I raised the gun and shot without ever being conscious of the sight picture or the safety. Feathers flew and the bird curved right out of the trees into the field where I fired again — still so deep in a shooter's trance I had no idea but that I was the gun, the shot, the bird. This time the bird turned over and fell straight down. We emerged from the wood — actually, I ran — to see it lying still over clipped hay. I took myself firmly in hand. "*Find* the bird, *dead* bird, Bart, *dead* bird." He was running joyously amok up and down the field. Once he stopped above the bird, gave a deep snort, then ran on. Finally, I picked it up myself: my first woodcock in seven years, velvety blacks, leaf-mold browns, moth-soft patterns, hard narrow whistling primaries. For this moment, home again.

■

The story doesn't end there. For the next two weeks I went out with the dogs: Mark Black's Ben, Eric Wilcox's Parker, and, above all, Bart. The two yearling setters were the epitome of stylish grace. They were as goofy as any spaniel—in Parker's case perhaps more so—until the scent of bird knocked them back in their tracks like a punch to stand firm, barely trembling. ("Whoa there, Parker. *Whoa*, Ben. Easy there. *Whoa!*") Then the whir and whirl of the flush, the brown blur seeking a hole in the tall riverine canopy, the shot and fall. And finally their version of "hunt dead," ending with another rigid point, head lower this time, and the magic of the lovely camouflaged bird materializing two feet off the dog's nose: "*Good* dog."

All as pretty as could be. Still, the joy of going after childhood's birds with my own dog surpassed even the setter's art. To the purist's surprise, he gave just as much warning as the pointing dogs did with his flash points, furiously wagging flag, sniffing, and nose-down wriggling. And he found downed birds, too—including a couple of stinking days-dead carcasses that nobody was willing to claim. But one fault persisted: He would not pick up the woodcocks.

I shot several three-bird limits, finding to my mild surprise that I was seeking them. On my final day I shot one and picked it up, as had become my habit, after Bart sniffed at it—or more properly snorted, as though he would inhale it. I barely even bothered with my usual, "Fetch it here!"

Then we came to a fallen tree and he began to wiggle. I barely had a chance to think "bird" before this one flushed, over and away. I fired but could not see whether I had hit a thing. Bart charged forward at the shot and disappeared around the tangle of branches. I followed to see him rooting around under a bush a good thirty yards to one side.

I gave a pro forma, resigned, "Fetch." He raised his head and ran straight at me, skidded to a stop on his bottom, eyes bulging and ears laid back, gums bared, a woodcock clenched rather too tightly in his teeth; trembling all over, shaking the bird, saying, perhaps, "*This* right? *This* fetch? *This* bird?"

I took his offering from his mouth; gave him a biscuit; spread the bird's wings. He tried to reclaim it then fell to quartering, his whole attitude transformed. I was allowed one more bird that day. But I took out the shells, crashed out of the woods, and called my dog to heel, giving him another biscuit for good measure. The next day I was flying to Albuquerque, en route to my chosen home in the back country. It seemed right to end the past just so.

Shooting Sportsman (1989)

Why Grouse?

The pheasant is the jeweled dragon of midwestern cornfields, brilliant in armored red and gold and oil-slick purple. He goes straight up over your springer, announcing himself with that gagging crow, big enough that you'd think you'd never miss but for your racing heart, that trailing, diverting tail. In your hand he is as fierce and edged as a gamecock.

Ducks fall in flocks from leaden skies of winter. You pay for ducks, with pain in your cold hands that surpasses numbness, with a dead spot at the end of your spine, with deep chills that neither your truck's heater nor three bourbons in front of the fire can touch; perhaps most, at least on the windless days when nothing moves, with that boredom that affects all denizens of our overstimulated culture when nothing happens. Yet dead, ducks are heavy and tangible, pregnant with the promise of rich dinners. Their plush grays and whites, touched with splashes of liquid color as vivid as beetles' wings, inspire artists; the finest always paint them as dead game, leaving the elusive wild bird to the hubris of calendar makers.

Geese and cranes, flying crosses with stretched trombone necks, wander in their Vs and long lines down Arctic flight lanes, creaking and yelping as they go. The wildfowler, most melacholy of hunters with his taste for stormy skies, hears them and thinks that he can hear all the sadness of distance and separation, of lost mates (these birds are faithful for life, unlike us), of places visited once, places at the ends of continents, places that he will never see, in their stuttering songs.

The little snipe, the "goat of the bogs," is touched with witchcraft. He does not breed where you live but springs up from the grass one morning like an animated toadstool, depositing a splash of white, and buzzes off in zigzags, low over the grass, crying. You will not see him again till next year. The woodcock, with huge eyes in an upside-down skull, is another magic-touched migrant. He arrives on moonlit nights. If you flush him, he burrs up with a twitter of wings, turns into a moth at treetop level, and disappears. If you miss him, he's gone down the wind's road tomorrow, following the cellular map locked in a brain smaller than those eyes.

Bobwhites are to the American as red grouse are to the English. They are the Tory bird, the social shooter's grail. If you do it right you hunt behind muscular, beetle-browed pointers that, when they stand, seem sculpted in stone. Your gun is a side-by-side double, never new, no larger than 20 bore (unless it was your grandfather's English 16). You may ride a horse with a gait as smooth as sprung wheels, or follow the dogs in a mule wagon. You are never alone, but accompanied by peers, handlers, servants for man and dog. You call your quarry "bird" as though there were no other. All is part of a ceremony as elegant and ordered and changeless as the old Latin Mass.

Even the western grouse have a unique and dramatic setting: They live in the sky. On the Plains, whether wheatfield edge or sage-brush flat, you stand in the sky as though you walked on the ocean's surface. The weather is all around you; the only thing taller than you in the whole sweep of 360 degrees is a windmill. It seems impossible to find a flock of birds in this immensity, and when you do, when they flush, it seems fitting that they disappear over the horizon, swinging left and right but never alighting before they mingle with the floaters in your eyes and disappear.

I hunt these birds, and love them all. So why, seven seasons after I shot the last one, am I haunted by the ruffed grouse? This past fall I was back in what is or at least was grouse country. But my old coverts were empty, with condos springing up on their edges like malignant growths. I found woodcocks in the riparian forest along the Saco River, and had what anyone would call a good season. But I now sit by the fire in a village adobe in the southern Rockies. Above the stucco walls and mud roads of the village rise snowy peaks and rolling plains, full of a variety and number of animals that I only dreamed of in my youth . . . three quails, turkeys, bandtails and doves, blue grouse, pintails, cinnamon teals, snow geese, sandhill cranes, coyotes and hares, antelope and elk and bears and cougars. So why do I sit by the fire and dream of ruffed grouse as though they were a lost love?

Part is personal, always. Outdoor writers are too fond of the so-called pathetic fallacy: "the clouds weep" and such. Those geese crying in the night are not sad; if there's a human equivalent, it's something between the exhortations of a rowing coxswain and the gabble of a bunch of people calling out to stay together in the dark. So of course grouse and nostalgia are linked for any hunter by their association with fall and its temporary death; by me, particularly, because they were the first upland bird I shot, though curiously, I don't recall which of the several remembered times was first. Perhaps more because I introduced my late partner, Betsy, to hunting through grouse. That one I remember: I flushed it out of an old orchard; fired; it towered; I fired again and it fell. They were my first two shots of the season, and he was a cock with a golden sheen above the powder black of his ruff. But I took Betsy after the grouse because above ducks and pheasants and grouse, they were already my chosen quarry.

So why grouse? Why do they flush through so many hunters' memories? Why do they attract more serious and reflective and, probably, romantic hunters than other birds?

They are of what only can be called medium size, a solid handful, but not a trophy like a pheasant or turkey or goose—not bursting with autumn ripeness like a duck.

Their habitat is far from wilderness; in real wilderness, except in old burns, you will never see a ruffed grouse—and in those places he will be tame and stupid. The sportsman's grouse is born of an evanescent ecology, where old fields have neither grown up to turkey woods nor been replaced by suburbs. To get grouse you need food plants— aspen and birch, feral apple, bayberry, juniper.

And for those grouse to be *real* grouse, grouse to persist forever in a sportsman's memory, you need enough hunting pressure over, maybe, a century to prune away the genes for stupid or trusting or whatever it is that makes wilderness grouse walk in circles on the ground while you watch, or fly into a tree twenty feet away to gawk and gabble at your dog. And yet you can't have legions of grimly determined yuppie grousers in new fashionable gunning togs and restocked Parkers pursuing their numerical goals into February. An invasion of northern goshawks will leave more seed stock than nouveaux gunners who worship numbers. Maybe we are losing "real" grouse, a sort of serendipitous, accidental by-product of history, as we lose their once-in-an-era habitat, the one that also produced, for one century, the grouse worshipers of whom I am a late example.

Meanwhile grouse are homebodies. They make no romantic journeys. You are likely to find them in the same place at the same time on any day. When they flush they may seem to disappear, but really they never go a quarter mile. Come back in an hour and you'll flush them again.

They are not vocal, and sing no songs of distant places. Their "song," rarely sung in the autumn, sounds like a ball bouncing to rest on a hardwood floor, or a distant chain saw. They make it by whirring their wings.

Their meat is delicate and pinkish white. It is not as instantly recognizable and strong as blood-rare roast duck, close to the bone, and does not demand as fierce a red wine. If you cook it too long, it's as dry as wood pulp. If you follow some of the recipes in so-called game cookbooks, breasting it out and simmering it for twelve hours with beans, it loses all character and tastes like—well, wet cardboard with beans. You must roast it whole and lightly, pick your wine, and serve it with, say, wild rice, to appreciate it.

Grouse are subdued in plumage; they show no one color but endless subtleties of gray and rust and cream. Their tail bars may gleam with copper; the ruff on an old male may be touched with iridescence or with a black so velvety and light absorbing that it resembles the gills beneath an old mushroom. Who alive can paint a grouse? Most imitations are hard edged and garish, standing out from the background like no live bird does. A still grouse is made of leaves. A few artists come close. Ogden Pleissner did the grouse in motion, the grouse fleeing through its chosen habitat. So does Chet Reneson. For a close-up, only Canada's George MacLean can build his bird of leaves and mushrooms and old velvet. I only wish the great Swede Bruno Liljefors had known American birds. His courting *Capercaillie*, creatures of the twilight forest floor, make me believe he would have a grouse of pigment and light that would trick and delight the hunter's eye.

And all these "grouse are nots" and "grouse have nots" are, of course, among the grouse's virtues—hand size, evanescent, subtle, inhabiting the vanishing remnants of childhood's landscapes. But there is more. Grouse demand skill in shooting, persistence, the discipline to walk and clamber and claw through thickets. Fancy guns may be de rigueur for bobwhites, but to shoot grouse well demands an almost biological coevolution of man and gun. The grouse gunner does not necessarily need a Purdey, rather either the willingness to find a gun that fits and points as effortlessly as the eye follows the fleeing bird, or else the determination to make the gun fit him—despite the gasps of "investors" and collectors who will malign him for despoiling shooting "art." I, like many faithless youths, long followed the first course through a roller coaster of gun lust and trading mania. These days I have a gun that fits, a 20-gauge Darne, and will never let it go. Others, older and wiser, chose the second way.

And one more thing we all know: Grouse are exciting. No. Grouse are more than exciting: They are a rush, a blast of adrenaline straight through the nerves to the heart. *Nothing* flushes like a ruffed grouse. If you see him on the ground, you can't follow him into the air. Most likely you don't see him; he crouches invisible, a creature of leaves, then roars out of your eye. In that whir of wings you must mount and follow and fire without knowing when or how you do so. It is as pure an act, an act as pure as thought, as a human can do, a kind of ecstacy in action. If you miss once you may fire again, but by then you are trying consciously and I, at least, usually miss. But if you fire straight and your quarry thumps to the ground, perhaps to run down, flying in its death throes for an eternal moment, you know both the joy and the sadness of hunting and maybe, even for a moment, of life and death. Zen and the art of grouse gunning? I know little of Zen, but I do know that grouse bring me all of this.

Shooting Sportsman (1988)

My Shotguns

There are guns for sports and guns for games. The guns for sports are better. Sporting clays is a game.

I'm a poor man who will shoot only good guns—and by "good" I mean aesthetic as well as functional. Years ago I formulated my thesis: Who wants to shoot a beautiful bird with an ugly gun? Despite poverty, I've stuck to my credo. If I can do it, anybody can.

A few principles first. That we are talking doubles here will come as a surprise to no one. Show a nonhunter (or an antihunter, even) a classic side-by-side next to an over-and-under or a repeater and he will pick the double every time. The answer will be even more emphatic if the critic is also an artist, architect, or engineer.

I would like to believe that the real hunter-aesthete is someone who moves, not someone who gets out of the car and says, "I have to *walk* over there?" But even if your game—dove, waterfowl, turkey—demands a blind, you want a wand, not a club. Like yourself, your gun should be lean and aerobic.

Side-by-sides got to be as good as they are the same way we and our sporting quarries did: evolution. Darwin figured it out in animals, but Augustus Henry Lane-Fox Pitt-Rivers, an eccentric English colonel and anthropologist in the nineteenth century, was the first to realize that such hybrid productions of mind and metal as machines evolve, too. Although he based his case on the British army rifle, Pitt-Rivers might have made an even better argument from the great Victorian flowering of sporting shotguns. From the 1860s to about World War I, English shotgun designs quickly mutated from muzzleloading guns, then became more efficient by bringing their hammers inside. Better (meaning cheaper to build, not necessarily stronger) steel barrels replaced baroque Damascus twists. Giant 4 bores were built for wildfowling, while more efficient powders made it possible to build smallbores for ladies and children. There may have been more gunmakers in Victorian England alone than exist in the world today.

The so-called best guns arose between 1870 and 1880—Purdey sidelocks, Westley Richards boxlocks and Dixon round actions that function so well today, they could exchange parts with contemporary guns by the same makers. Even with competition and cheap labor, such guns were not cheap, but neither were their prices absurdly high. Now they cost considerably more than my little house in New Mexico.

In the United States, although most guns were machine made, similar designs soon evolved, such as the Fox, which was as light and elegant as any British or Continental gun. But after World War II, with costs rising, many Americans turned their backs on doubles—they were old-fashioned and cost too much. One good one, the Winchester Model 21, continued to be built, but it was always expensive and usually bulky. Poor Americans with a taste for game guns were limited to some elegant Spanish doubles of uncertain reliability, Belgian knockabouts, and, for brief periods, the French Darne. English guns back then cost over a thousand dollars; although the prices seem absurdly cheap now, that was a lot more money when you could get a hand-finished, Belgian-built Browning Superposed for four hundred.

Although the Superposed is a beautifully made gun, I blame it more than any other design for ruining the American taste in doubles.

It had good wood, hand engraving, fine checkering, a perfect metal fit—and a profile somewhere between a pregnant whale's and a two-by-four's. The Superposed imprinted its image upon a generation of hunters who never got to know anything better, and from the 1960s onward, the gun spawned a legion of reasonably priced imitations made in Japan. Now its influence extends to England. Is this because it's better? I'd argue that it's evolution again—for sporting clays.

For such games, weight is an asset, and the so-called single-sighting plane is better designed for getting a little more peripheral vision than for pointing. But if you are among the perhaps-dwindling minority who still likes to hunt wild birds in wild surroundings, you might want to think the whole thing through for a little longer. Yes, such weighty guns will work well on shooting preserves, too, if you like going to the supermarket. Forgive me, but this is shopping, not hunting. Artificial situations are always less demanding.

Consider instead: Light weight, within limits, is a virtue when you are hacking through alder jungles or climbing up nine-thousand-foot ridges. Still, you want a fair amount of shot, and 20s just aren't that versatile. A 12, however, that weighs just over six pounds, can shoot up to 1⅛ ounces comfortably. Nor are you much disadvantaged by the 16, with one ounce of shot. It's surprising how many English 16s were owned by soldiers and naturalists and other travelers in rough places.

The barrel should be long and light—not the 32-inch cannons of wildfowl guns, but at least 27½, a common European length. Twenty-six-inch tubes seem to wave themselves around. Twenty-fives are unspeakable. A lot of old doubles, at least those from across the Atlantic, have thirty-inch barrels that weigh less than three pounds—perfect. Long barrels swing smoothly, even if you are winded, and light ones carry well.

Wood? I'm a fan of English-style straight grips on everything: I find them more versatile and quicker to mount from a low carry, the obverse of the hooked pistol grips on clays guns. On beavertails I'm actually agnostic: Slim ones, as found on old Parkers and Model 21s of 16 gauge or under, work fine and provide a bit of weight forward.

Stock length is my one mild disagreement with English orthodoxy. I shoot a long (14½-inch-plus) stock best in good conditions, but a slightly shorter one might work best on an all-around rough-country gun; it adjusts to more conditions.

As for the action—well, the classic boxlock can't be beat. It's marginally stronger in the wrist than a sidelock (less wood is removed) and usually much cheaper. The closest American approximation is the Fox, recently revived (though so far only in a 20—let's see a 16). If you can find an old French Darne with its weird sliding breech, you'll have a jewel: light and strong, with wonderful lines.

The gun that has all of these features—for hunting grouse in the East, bobwhite quail in the swamps, sage birds in the flats, and Mearns' in the mountains—is, precisely, the British-style game gun as it was made for the servants of the Empire (maybe with a slightly shortened stock). Such guns were pruned back in the era between the World Wars, by the Depression and changing tastes. They are making a modest comeback now, which pleases me.

I am not talking the thirty-thousand-dollar Purdeys and Bosses here. I am talking about a spread of guns from the plain honest Precision Sports game guns (made by Ugartechea in Spain) through various small-framed Parkers, smallbore Foxes, overlooked Darnes, battered Francotte knockabouts from Abercrombie & Fitch, lightweight LCs, William Evans 16s, and late-Empire boxlocks from small Birmingham makers like Pape and Ford. The top end of this range is still around three thousand dollars—for something you'll use for a lifetime if you treat it right, something pretty enough to look at when you're not using it.

My William Evans 16, which I acquired (in partial barter) for less than you think, is a perfect example. It has what one shotgun aesthete calls "erotic wood," a deep orangey brown with contrasting black streaks, almost invisibly fine rose-and-scroll engraving covering an action body worn silvery by its hundred-plus years, and the sweeping lines unchanged since the eighteenth-century genius Joe Manton perfected them. It weighs just shy of six pounds despite its thirty-inch, still "in-proof" barrels of velvety (not shiny) black. It is as deadly as it is beautiful.

To look at, to swing at imaginary birds, and, yes, to fondle. The same evolutionary pressure that made side-by-sides efficient made them beautiful, giving them what Thomas McGuane, who loves such guns, described as a "simple linear gesture." (All right, he was talking about his flats skiff, but the principle counts!) Such a gesture, executed in plain metal, exceeds in beauty any gold-inlaid monstrosity without the look.

Remember, you go out to kill beautiful birds with this thing, not just shoot it at clay Frisbees. A sweeter tool will make you a better shot. You'll get out more, walk longer and higher, see more country. As the feedback between you and your gun continues, you will become a better hunter, shaped by the coevolutionary pressure of your good gun. I won't say you'll become a better person, be kinder to your dog, or be a better game cook. But stranger things have happened.

Sports Afield (1994)

Evolution of a Hunter

The first time I took Libby Frishman bird hunting was a memorable occasion.

It was opening day of the grouse season, four seasons back. We had been keeping company for almost a year then. Libby came from a background more inclined to mountain climbing than hunting. Her father was an early Sierra Club member who pioneered routes in Yosemite Valley, and Sherpas visited her childhood home in the Bay area. She did grow up fly fishing (she actually fishes casts or wets, which establishes her firmly as prefaddish) but, although her late husband, Harry, shot her mother's inherited Parker, she had never killed any wild birds herself. Still, with a devotion to all things culinary and outdoors, she was ready to go September first.

We decided on a ridge in the Tobacco Roots; we knew there were blue grouse there, and our friend Jane keeps a cabin with its own private hot spring in the canyon below, to soothe our aching middle-aged bones after a two-thousand-foot ascent and descent. We left early and slogged up through meadows and an intermittent stream. Bart the springer flushed a snipe, but we saw no grouse that morning.

Blues were new to me. I had grown up on ruffed grouse in the East—where they don't fly into trees—but had spent most of the last twenty years chasing running southwestern quail, shooting doves, ambushing bandtailed pigeons, and crouching in blinds for snow geese. I didn't know the rhythms or even the exact habitat of blue grouse.

We began getting into them late that afternoon, on long, sloping grassy ridges that ran down into towering firs. The first ones confused Bart. As he nosed them up they erupted like "normal" birds and flew immediately up into the trees. He sat and looked, distressed. This was against the rules.

I felt the same way. "Throw a stick at them, will you?" I maneuvered around to get a clear shot, then looked back at Libby, who had not only not picked up a stick but was also staring at me with what looked like disbelief.

"Why?"

"To make them fly."

She still looked dubious. "If they're too dumb to fly, why make it hard on yourself?"

A dozen answers about sport and wingshooting died in my throat. I had just run up against, at the risk of seeming sexist, the deepest issue that divides male and female hard-core woodspersons: the rock-bottom, unsentimental pragmatism of the female hunter confronted with something edible.

After a moment she apparently decided to indulge my silly male whims. She flung a stick up into the branches. The first one wouldn't fly. The second did, and I missed it, causing both Libby and Bart to groan. On my third opportunity, I sinned: When the silly damn bird wouldn't fly, I shot it off the limb. Bart pounced, retrieved it, and sat, grinning. Libby's expression was not dissimilar.

After a soak in Jane's plunge and a first bottle of red wine I didn't feel too guilty. After the bird, and a second bottle, I didn't feel guilty at all. Still, I had learned something about sex roles and hunting: If women are not affected by Bambiism, they are a lot more practical then men. Or as John Barsness once said about his wife, the noted writer Eileen Clarke: "The first five sage grouse she shot were all ground-sluiced. They had skid marks on their breasts."

∎

Lib's fascination with bird hunting—"a walk in the country with your dogs, birding, and a great meal at the end"—continued to grow. On a late-season safari east of Lewistown we all hunted hard, but on the third subzero day only three of us finished the hunt: publisher Chuck Johnson, Libby, and me. She was still grinning and looking for the next bird when everybody else was in watching the ball game and even aging Bart was *hors de combat*. Chuck gives no quarter, and he praised her grit.

That spring we started weekend clays shoots at our friend Tim's. Tim is a genial sporting squire with an amazing collection of guns—not an ostentatious one, but one that is scholarly, almost museum quality. We fooled around with a dozen gunstocks until we found one that fit her. It was an unusually short one, from a nineteenth-century rook rifle; Lib, though she is tall, has a stiff neck from being run down by a hit-and-run driver when she was guiding in Nepal twenty years ago.

Without telling her, I went looking for "her" gun. It would be a light 20 gauge, a double to please the eye, with a short stock. I mentioned this to another friend, Datus, and he came out of his back room with a 5½-pound prewar Belgian 20 with a thirteen-inch stock. It had been made for a lady and came complete with a leather trunk case. We shook hands, and that Christmas it became Libby's gun for life. Her friend Joanne, who doesn't even like guns, admired its bouquets of rose-and-scroll engraving and told her she should get a lace sleeve to complement it and carry it in.

She's getting deadly now. She and Eileen and some others have taken up clays shooting at the Logan Gun Club with Dave Gentry, an inspired teacher. She found that although she liked the short stock, it had a tendency to bruise her finger, so she got a rubber extension pad. Now she can smoke targets without flinching.

But a certain pragmatism remains. When we were last in Magdalena I overheard her talking to Christine, another woman who doesn't understand the moral necessity of making a bird fly, about shooting running blue quail. They don't even look embarassed. We still open our season every fall on that high ridge above Jane's place, with a bottle of red and a hot pool waiting. But I suspect that any bird that doesn't fly won't live to regret it.

Big Sky Journal (1996)

Old Dog

No, this isn't going to be one of those sentimental "I-knew-an-old-dog-who-died" stories. For one thing, Bart, black-and-white springer, is very much alive. If I take down the dog barrier in the door to my library, he'll be here in an instant, flipping my hand up with his nose, pawing me incessantly. He means two things by this: Pay attention to me! (Not to those young dogs.) And: Let's go. Birds. Hunting.

The thing is, he's old. *Very* old, by some standards. He'll be fourteen in February. His long life has spanned human and animal disasters and triumphs, the publishing of my first book, widowhood, divorce, a new marriage. One of his puppyhood's companions, my old "staghound" Riley, son of a coursing greyhound sire and a Scottish deerhound dam, died of old age five years ago. In his prime he was the scourge of jackrabbits and coyotes, running them down by sheer speed and energy, but he died in his sleep at nine, his great heart and legs broken down by his size and the strains of his profession. That whole canine generation is gone—rattlers, debilitating diseases, disappearance, even once the bullets of some subhuman jerk without a trace of a good dog's nobility. The big back country of southwestern New Mexico can be hard on dogs and people.

Bart has hunted quail here, always; pheasants and blue grouse (he didn't like their habit of treeing) in Montana; ducks everywhere, and, for one season's exile, woodcocks in Maine. He had to live in a kennel there and hated it, though he loved the smelly little woodsnipes once he realized they were dog-legal game.

But when we went out after grouse after a September snowstorm in Montana, I thought he had reached the end of his hunter's road. The cover, willow and aspen, ran up a narrow drainage, from cropland to dark timber, on the west side of a mountain range near Bozeman. Although you could often raise four or five flushes there the woods remained silent as the last flakes sifted down. Bart started valiantly, snorting and dislodging snow from low-hanging branches. Five minutes uphill he began trudging, and his tail began to hang low. In ten minutes he lay down to bite snowballs from between his toes. In fifteen, for almost the first time in his life, he was walking behind me, letting me break trail. When I realized that was what he wanted, I let him.

He surged in front only once, when a yearling black bear feeding on rotting apples galumphed away like a cross between a black Lab and a beach ball. Bart swerved around me to give chase, as he had in the past for—once each—a coyote and a mountain lion. He's nearly deaf now, and it took more than a couple of bellows to call him back. When he returned he got in line behind me again, stopping periodically to chew the ice on his feet. I figured that the aging process, which we first acknowledged when he collapsed on the third day of a midwinter pheasant hunt east of Grassrange, was complete, and he would now spend his shortening days sleeping on my bed or in front of the stove.

Right after that hunt Lib and I married and moved to my old house in Magdalena, where Bart had been born under the desk that held my late partner, Betsy's, word processor. The old dog seemed to respond to the New Mexico sun. Though it's often cold at sixty-five hundred feet he stopped begging to come in. He spent hours basking, lying in the soft dry dirt in front of the hawk's perch. He stopped growling at the dachshund pup, and—not entirely intelligently—began challenging Bo, the two-year-old Aussie with the glaring blue-marble left eye.

Still, the quail habitat around Magdalena seemed too rugged for an old dog's legs, ranging as it does from six to eight thousand feet, all rocky and vertical and covered with cholla and goat's head seeds and lechiguilla beneath its grass and oaks and piñons. The move and its attendant complications had caught us without a successor for Bart; besides, there are hawks to train, a yard to be refenced, kennels and lofts and mews to build. I decided to teach Bo to be an interim bird dog. He was intelligent and knew "fetch"; his father, Jedediah, flushed quarry for his owner's hawk; he was curious about the sound of the gun and not a bit gun shy. Besides, our mountain hunting is of a rough-and-ready kind; in the same cover we can flush Gambel's quail, occasional scalies, and Mearns' in good years. Nor do we scorn cottontails or hares. Past teams have included such combinations as two springers and a saluki, or a springer, a shooter, and a hawk.

For practice, we took the old dog and the young one to the abandoned dirt-track airfield just north of town, where the quail were never shot and so multiplied even in dry years. In fifteen minutes we were into a big early-season flock; thirty, perhaps even forty birds. Bo leaped about, ecstatic, giving chase like a sighthound. He had never been praised for chasing anything before. Bart didn't even spare the energy for disgust. He was doing what he was born to do, flagged half tail whirling like a propeller, nose low, snorting like a pig. As Bo raced up and down the track like a mad thing Bart crossed and recrossed in the rabbit brush, nosing out single after double after single. He was wide awake and alive, though he kept giving us puzzled looks. Why weren't we *shooting?*

■

Bart is hunting again. I could end this, neatly and conventional-
ly, by telling you the detailed story of his and Bo's first gun hunt in
New Mexico. Of how they nosed out a fat young cottontail in the
junipers, and how I snap-shot instinctively with the French gun. Of
how I was sure that I had connected and so sent Bo, the nearer dog, to
fetch. Of how he didn't come back. Of how Libby finally went in to
find Bo standing in puzzlement and, to be fair, fascination over a dead
bunny on the clean sand. And of how Bart, grumbling under his
breath, shouldered aside the strong young macho and picked up the
rabbit to deliver it to my hand, his slightly foggy eyes rolling in his head
like marbles, the way they always do.

But that's not an end, not the point. Bart is hunting again, two
times, three times a week. At almost fourteen, he still has the fire. His
nose—his "turbo sniffer," as Libby calls it—still drinks in the scent
despite the lost cells of the aging process and two rattler bites. Bo is
back guarding the yard and helping friends round up cattle.

It's late afternoon, and I'm tired and sweated out. My slightly
arthritic right knee aches, and I'm passing the light double gun from
hand to hand. I want to lean on a tree and rest.

But look at that old dog! He's been hunting for five hours now,
going from morning's frost to dry heat, snuffling through rocky arroyos,
up and down and up again, from six thousand feet up to sixty-five,
down to fifty-five, and back up again. We've moved one covey of Gambel's, a four-point buck, a black-tailed jackrabbit, and an eagle. Sure,
he's rested a few times in the shade (he often digs a little and lies on
his belly in the cool disturbed earth), and he's soaked himself to the
skin in a cattle tank, swimming as he drinks. Still, his tail, docked at
two-thirds length rather than a show dog's stub, waves high, flagging
his progress through the thorny scrub.

We're nearly to the truck. I'm inclined to call it a day. I tell myself
that I don't want to wear Bart out. He's been slowing down a bit for the
last half hour, returning from his forays to walk at heel for a few paces,

something he could never bring himself to do when he was young. My focus has been drifting, too; I'm daydreaming, and if a quail was to get up, I'd probably fumble the gun and miss it. And why hunt if you're not intense; why hunt at all?

We both see the truck at the same time. Bart stands in the path for a moment, staring, then wags his tail and leaps off the path into the brush-choked arroyo on my left. His turbo sniffer activates, his tail begins to vibrate. He noses under a cholla, emerges, picks a goat's head from his foot, and goes on, directly away from the truck.

See? He's still hunting. I unscrew the cap of my canteen, take a long swallow and a deep breath, and mount my gun more firmly. There are birds out there, tantalizing smells, adventures over the next hill. "Find the birds, Bart. *Find* 'em."

Forthcoming (1997)

A Long Way
from Home

I didn't move to my perch on the edge of the Magdalena Mountains
in southwestern New Mexico for the trout fishing. But it's where I
do much of my fishing now. As Thomas McGuane wrote in *The Heart
of the Game*, "Hunting in your own back yard becomes with time, if
you love hunting, less and less expeditionary."

What I don't want to do here is reinforce coastal prejudices about
what kind of place the high plateaus here are. (Or then again, maybe
I do; I mean, I don't want you to *move* here.) This is important: I *do
not live in the desert*. Easterners in particular seem to think that the
Southwest is like Phoenix without swimming pools—hundred-plus-
degree temperatures, saguaro cacti, bare rock mountains, all-terrain
vehicles, warm winters, sleepy Mexicans, taciturn cowboys, nuclear
tests, Edward Abbey . . . you can name your own clichés.

If you are to understand fly fishing here, you must understand
what manner of place I inhabit.

First, it's high country. If you leave the Rio Grande valley at
Socorro to take the only paved road west in a stretch of approximately 125 miles of state highway—the only way to get to Magdalena—you

start your climb to the edge of the Rio's rift at an altitude of forty-five hundred feet above sea level.

Then you go up for twenty-six miles—steeply for the first half, then up an incline so slow it almost seems you are driving across a brown pool table. When you top out at the beginning of this subtly inclined part, you have already reached six thousand feet in altitude; by the time you reach Magdalena you will have added another five hundred.

To your left, if it is winter, the Magdalenas look like the Alps, their jagged peaks covered with snow. They should: South Baldy, the highest peak, almost achieves eleven thousand feet. If you live in Magdalena, you live on a dry grassy plain that is the same height as the tallest mountain in my native New England, staring south at those Pleistocene peaks. Remember the adjective Pleistocene, and let me wander a little farther afield.

The second thing about this country—call it the Gila country for convenience—is that, even though it is cold and more likely to snow here in May or October than in Boston, it is dry. Oh, most winters you get a winter-long snowpack on the peaks that is deep enough to require snowshoes or cross-country skis. And when you venture up the mountain canyons in the spring, through meadows, under hundred-foot-tall ponderosas and Douglas firs (not a desert, remember?), you might think that the little stream cutting its way through the bottom would be ideal for small native trout.

But that's in April, when the snow is melting. Come back in June and the stream will have disappeared, leaving nothing but dry rocks and sand-rimmed puddles where, if you are very lucky, you may find the fresh print of an invisible mountain lion.

The stream will return, often bigger than it was in spring, after the daily thunderstorms of July and August. Sometimes, if it's a very wet year, it may flow, at least in a trickle, until winter freezes it solid.

What is going on here, besides modern cycles of drought or heat, is that these mountains have been slowly drying out since the time of

the last glaciation. If Folsom man had been a fly fisherman, he doubtless could have cast a fly over native cutthroats in Hop Canyon, not five
miles by air from my house. However, since he was still dealing with
imperial mammoths, oversize bison, saber-toothed cats, and dire wolves,
he may not have had the leisure to contemplate catch-and-release fishing. Yes, there were trout here once, and not that long ago, either.

The next thing to think about in this country is that it is very big.
There are enormous distances between very small towns, and to my
southwest four paved roads enclose an area bigger than Connecticut
that is inhabited by only twenty-seven hundred people. As you move
southwest in this block, the forested mountain ranges become bigger,
with smaller open plains between them. If you run along the pavement
on the eastern or southern edge, you will never see water except in the
Rio Grande, which, dozing under huge cottonwoods, is rather like the
Nile in miniature—static most of the year and intensely diverted to
agriculture. All the old tributaries that lead down to it are barren, dry
canyons—"sand rivers" that only flow in the spring or after thunderstorms. This, perversely, is a reason to treasure the high country.
Nobody goes there but locals—what could attract an interstate tourist
cruising Route 25 in his Winnebago to those distant blue mesas shim-
mering in the summer heat?

Well, for one thing, Canadian temperatures in July. And, for
another, trout. Native cutts, monster browns, stocked rainbows. The
Magdalenas, perched on the plateau's edge, are too narrow and too
exposed to hold enough water for permanent streams. Their next
neighbors to the southwest, the San Mateos, are lusher and probably
lost their trout later. But keep on pushing, almost against logic, to the
southwest. When you reach about one hundred miles in any of several bearings from Magdalena, you will find the true remnants of the
Pleistocene: blue spruce, willow, aspen. And streams. And more than
one kind of good fishing.

Somewhat arbitrarily, I call any water that I can reach by taking one paved road a piece of "home" water. By this definition there are three such points: Quemado Lake, the Rio Grande, and the San Francisco River. And since Quemado Lake is—well, I'll tell you in a moment—I'll add one more, one I can reach by way of a 125-mile *unpaved* road: Willow Creek, which in its modest way may be the best of all.

■

Quemado Lake is a high-country impoundment about ninety miles from Magdalena that can be reached by way of the main highway, a picturesque two-lane that travels across the Continental Divide and through three tiny towns. Although it is man-made, it is "pretty"—a still, blue cup surrounded by tall ponderosas. All my neighbors go there for what they call trout fishing.

Now I am far from a fly snob or, for that matter, a trout snob; I have written elsewhere of my love for catfish and live bait. But for me, the method and (what I hate to call) the ambience have to be appropriate to the quarry. I don't ground-sluice prairie chickens, hunt sparrows with my peregrine falcon, or use my 10 bore for Mearns' quail.

At Quemado, there is a parking lot. Half of it is usually full of trailers and RVs. The fishermen and -women, many of them friends of mine, sit in chairs along the lakeside with two or more spinning rods propped beside them. The preferred baits are Velveeta and "fireballs." The trout are often sixteen inches long, grain-fed piscine cattle, and, you know, I'd just as soon go to the Safeway. It's only twenty-six miles away, and freezing doesn't seem to do too much to harm the taste of hatchery fish that are so slow witted and voracious they seem to spend no more than a week in the little lake's artificial "freedom." I suspect they're *scared* of insects.

And even if they aren't, fly fishing for such fish is preposterous. You can't dignify supermarket fishing by using fancy tools. My friends have the right idea.

So, ascending: the Rio Grande. I don't use the fly rod much on the Big River, either. Whether the Rio is a "natural" river is a moot question, but it *is* full of fish, large and small, of many species, all wild. My favorite quarries there are monster catfish, and tying a fly to mimic a ten-inch salamander would be an odd proposition, even if I owned a rod heavy enough to cast it. Still, there are times in the spring when you can take a boat up into the flooded cottonwoods, where the river begins to give way to the head of Elephant Butte Reservoir, and imagine yourself to be in some Deep South bayou, minus the alligators and most of the mosquitoes. You can take the 8-weight Fenwick and some hairy poppers made from the hair of last year's deer and entice splashy strikes from largemouth bass guarding their beds. Or you can take a handful of old shad flies that first saw service on Massachusetts tidal streams a decade past and work the runoff-swollen ditches for gleaming metallic yellow bass that are like tiny, deep-bodied, lemon stripers. (For that matter, the Montana painter, writer, and angler Russell Chatham insists that someday we will take a boat and penetrate Elephant Butte's immense reaches, where we will refine saltwater fly-fishing techniques for stripers and transform "desert" reservoir fishing. I'll do it, when the time comes. But there's something purely shocking to a kid who grew up in the last glory days of the New England striper surf to *see* a striped bass in New Mexico, never mind catch one on a fly.)

So, back to the high country again, a hundred and more miles west into the plateau, to the San Francisco, one of the Gila River's headwaters. This is pure New Mexico fly fishing, right down the middle. Which is to say it's good, it's consistent, the fish are big, and it looks, as they say here, *real different*. For instance: rock walls, often more than a hundred feet high, over the stream. There are few trees except on sandbars, and those mostly willows and young cottonwoods that will be swept away in the next flood, or tropical-looking walnuts hung with curtains of wild grapes in the rare broad stretches.

But also: roaring water, deep holes, the energizing smell of wet air. And birds everywhere: familiar, tipsy spotted sandpipers; tropical tanagers and Scott's orioles like Christmas ornaments; vermillion flycatchers like coals from the woodstove that snap up insects in repetitive motions, mechanical-toy predators; swallows looping, like crosses between falcons and dragonflies; herons groaning in protest, lumbering into the air, then levitating upstream.

And fish! I fish streamers here, and Woolly Buggers, and big hairy nymph-type deals I tie myself. With them, I catch nice rainbows and the occasional killer brown. Also, to my entire delight, smallmouth bass, which I have been in love with since I lived on the Saco River in Maine and caught them on minnow imitations trolled behind my canoe in the dusk. And once in a while—on the same flies—a muscular and graceful channel cat. While I stoutly maintain that it's an affectation to try to catch a catfish on a fly, I can't suppress a giggle of pleasure when I see one rolling in the wash with a fly designed for New England lakes dangling amid the whiskers. Variety is the spice of life— in the catching, as well as in the later, and most pleasing, eating.

■

But the best of my home waters, not in quantity or size or culinary reward, or almost anything but pure aesthetics, is this last: Willow Creek. I only get up there a couple of times a year because I'm busy and poor and it's a long, grueling four-wheel trip to the Gila's deep mountain stream. Still, that's best, too: I can remember how sick I got of a diet of stripers, quahogs, lobsters, and mussels—how occasionally tiresome even the rituals of obtaining them became—when I lived for a year in a one-room shack on the New England coast and of necessity did nothing but hunt and fish and gather and worry.

Willow Creek is caviar from the Caspian. It's tiny; you don't need waders. It's brushy and foggy and cold and surrounded by dank stands of fir and wet meadows full of rare, semiaquatic subspecies of garter snake. It looks as though it should have grizzlies, which indeed it should; we lost our last ones here in the thirties, and some inspired maniac should put them back.

There are a few stocked trout here, trickling down from a remote high-country lake. But the real fish here are eight-inch native cut-throats. Like most small-stream native trout, they resemble cloisonné ornaments and have deep red flesh. However, despite my unregenerate piscivory, I rarely keep one; they have a hard enough time surviving near-glacial winters and periodic, scouring floods. Come to think of it, though, they do a lot better here than the big, soft stockers, and they have been here a lot longer.

The fishing is unrefined by spring-creek standards. I use mostly terrestrials. Apart from being the natives' most natural summer food source, terrestrials delight me because they look like something real — a grasshopper, an ant, a beetle — without leading me down the tiresome and time-consuming path of hatch matching. And if your heart doesn't thrill to see one of these parakeet-brilliant little dinosaurs hit a perfect grasshopper on the surface with an audible *bap!* then you're not welcome to fish with me or brag about your fishing.

Are these my home streams forever? I don't know. They say there's some great fishing across the Big River near Ruidoso, where Sierra Blanca towers twelve thousand feet above real desert. But there are Texans there and condos and German elk hunters who pay five thousand dollars a head to shoot semitame elk. It's interesting, but I feel I leave my *querencia,* my heart's home, when I cross the Rio Grande.

Being that odd kind of homeless person that every writer is, I know that I might someday pull up stakes and go someplace where there are more trout, more grouse, and more water — Taos, maybe, where the Rio Grande resembles a monstrous version of the San Francisco, or even Montana, where a by-no-means-rich friend of mine just bought a place with a stream the size of Willow Creek running through it. I hear there is great falconry in Idaho, and steelhead on the borders. We won't even mention Provence, or Puglia, or Mongolia. . .

And yet I have something here, a whole life in a wild place, and things to do. My diverse enthusiasms, from Gila cutts to horses to gyrfalcons to books, and even New York City, can all be indulged here at the appropriate times. I do not envy the city-bound, even though they have more money than I, who fly to Iceland and Yellowstone to go fishing, and have more entertainment than I can find at the Golden Spur Bar. And I know some of them envy me. Here, a hundred miles from some of my home water, I have learned a few things that I cannot even wholly comprehend yet. One of them is that home, and home water, can be a long way from home.

Home Waters (1991)

The Catfish
Heretic

I want to sing the praises of a fish whose pursuit will never be chic. In an era when stockbrokers and Manhattan models dress themselves from the pages of the L. L. Bean catalog, when blue jeans cost more if they're partly worn out, some forms of outdoor recreation are more equal than others. The trout, for instance, has progressed from an already-high, establishment status to being *the* yuppie fish. Whereas the catfish, whether a hornpout the size of a bullfrog tadpole or a blue cat with the heft and docility of a Harley Davidson, is not going to make the cover of *Field & Stream*, let alone the columns of *Esquire*.

You can still talk about fly fishing in New York. It enjoys all kinds of comfortable associations—literary, gentlemanly, nostalgic. Successful writers fish for trout. I'm told that Mikhail Baryshnikov does. Even fashion magazines run four-color spreads on Hardy reels. Meanwhile, subliterate entrepreneurs use catfish to sell stinkbaits in the classified section of *Fur-Fish-Game*.

Catfish are socially unacceptable. Your basic trout angler stands in a glossy-magazine river idyll, sporting a military mustache, clothes by Ralph Lauren, vest by Orvis. His catfishing counterpart is a gap-toothed yokel in stained overalls with a cheek full of Red Man and a tractor cap, hoisting a slimy monster with all the presence of a feed sack full of bowling balls. If his picture appears at all, it's a grainy photo in the back pages of a Kansas weekly. As one salmonid snob said to me, "Ugly water, ugly fish, and not very beautiful people."

Don't get me wrong. I'm not here to apologize for mudcats. Nor do I wish to elevate catfishing by using fancy tools. It's just that, to me, the dark corners of sport are where essence and art still lurk.

I was raised right, as they say out here. I grew up near Boston doing all the correct things. I cast dry flies to rising fish, crawled up tunnel-like mountain streams after tiny native trout, waded shifty winter sandbars near the mouths of tidal rivers searching for "salters." I can (or could) lean an angled roll cast in under the overhanging lip of cedar in a blackwater swamp while simultaneously brushing away blackflies with my left hand, knowing that if I did everything just so, the bright line against the darkness would disclose a perfect brookie.

And then I moved to New Mexico. In the pools and ditches of the Rio Grande, I discovered catfish.

Some of my friends, especially easterners, say it's a case of "love the one you're with." You know, down there in the desert and all that, so far from the water, the poor bastard's gotta make do. But it's more complicated than that. Far more complicated. For one thing, New Mexico probably has more miles of blue-ribbon trout water than Massachusetts, full of bigger trout. Also, the catfish lurk forty miles away and two thousand feet below, steaming in the summer's heat.

I think it has more to do with the fact that, over the last twenty years, fly fishing has begun to make me nervous. It has become high tech and pseudoscientific, full of significant innovations that are immediately surpassed by even more significant innovations. Stream-side chatter is heavy on entomological Latin: People who didn't even know a mayfly from a mosquito ten years ago discourse on *Hexagenia* and *Baetis* in a cloud of pipe smoke. In fact, I fear that my old pastime has become the blood sport of urbanites and vegetarians, so refined that somebody who actually eats fish is considered to be as spooky and recidivist as a cannibal. Theirs is a sport that has no place for a piscivorous man with one old cane rod, an ancient Pflueger reel, and a firm attitude of "fish the Adams, ignore the hatch."

Bass fishing is even worse. Maybe it's still pursued by "good old boys"—but what kind of sport, for the poor romantic, is one that involves ten-thousand-dollar fishing machines and reels that look at best like someone sat on them, and at worst like ray guns? No, if we're going to get down to the essence of fishing, we're going to have to get down to bait—the truly organic lure—and catfish, whose only bard compared them to animated mud. Preferably big catfish.

I have to admit that I love to cast big live animals after big ugly predatory fish, to probe murky water with a necessarily stout rod on a slow river at night. And, unlike neighbors who prefer the rather bland white flesh of the catfish to anything else—personally, I was raised on bluefish—it's the fishing itself, bound up inextricably with its unique environment, that excites me. I still love fly fishing: the arc and curve and line and flex of it, its tools, finer than anything used in sport except possibly fine double shotguns. But there's something biological and smelly and wholly real about sitting down here in this beautiful nightmarish swampscape dangling a four-footed animal into another world, searching for something that scares divers.

Of course, you work up to this kind of thing in stages. In my case, I started by going out with neighbors. My recollection of that initiation is as warm, and as vivid, I think, as the impressions of any trout fisherman when he is first introduced to a gurgling New England brook.

We're sitting on a sandbank on the west side of the Rio Grande, maybe a quarter mile south of the San Acacia diversion dam. On the bridge over the dam you stand in a roar, with water cascading through the spillways in a standing wave that would smash you like a fly if you fell off the narrow catwalk. The air is full of swallows and oxygen, and the wet smell of life and decay. Upstream the river swings through flat-water bends and sandbars, with a promise of waterfowl in the fall. Downstream is a maze of riffles and waves, sandbars and drowned willows. You know that these holes and backwaters contain fish, thriving on the oxygen-rich water and the bounty of the stunned river creatures created by the dam.

This is theory. My friend Chubby Torres embodies practice and empirical knowledge, demonstrated by his laden stringer containing two fat little yellow bullheads and four channel cats ranging in size up to one that might go seven pounds. As we arrive his partner, Shirley, is skidding in another fish. It glows brilliant yellow as it turns belly up in the liquid silt. "Just a bullhead," says Chubby. "Throw it back. They taste muddy." Although I have eaten and enjoyed its relative, the black bullhead or hornpout, back East, I say nothing. I'm here to learn.

"Here's how you do it," coaches Chubby. "We use crappie rigs—room enough for two hooks and a little sinker at the end. Hook your worms through the collar so they oscillate in the current." Chubby is even more given to trisyllables than I am.

"Now cast upstream, reel in twice, and let the current take it." He suits his actions to his words. The line comes tight at about ninety degrees from the bank and swings downstream at a startling rate. "I let it go down until it fishes the hole right by that big rock. The fish get tired of fighting the strength of the current and look for slow places. I put my rod down, right here"—he leans the rod on a fallen cottonwood snag—"and wait. If it's a bullhead, it gives a hard tug. If it's a channel cat, it'll just give a nibble. I wait a minute and then hit it hard," says Chubby, striking an imaginary catfish so hard that his spin-casting rig bends double.

He seems to be right. Five minutes haven't passed when he takes the line up with his index finger, tests it for a moment, then makes another dramatic strike. This time the rod tip stays bent, vibrates, pulls down nearly to the water, and then up again. "These fish fight," Chubby explains, still in his teaching mode. In a couple of minutes he works it in close to the bank, a shining, popeyed creature with a spike dorsal and a Gorgon's snaky beard, wiggling in the mud like an amphibian. This one is eighteen inches long—no mere bullhead, but a real channel cat. "And they *are* good to eat."

I can now testify to that. I've caught two of the river's species of catfish so far—the scorned yellow bullhead and the channel cat, *Ictalurus punctatus.* The bullhead is an ungraceful, toadlike, rotund little creature, though with a brilliant canary yellow belly; I suspect its unpopularity has more to do with its ugliness and small size—usually about a foot long—than with its gustatory quality, though the books agree with Chubby that if not iced soon after capture, its flesh will be "mushy."

The channel cat, though just as likely a consumer of worms and stinkbaits and rotten chicken necks as its little cousin, will also take baitfish and lures and even—though I maintain that using them is a little pretentious—flies. It has obviously evolved to fight stronger currents than the bullhead, currents that have carved it into a classic gamefish profile. Channel cats are the number-one catfish of big rivers, commercial ponds, and southern fish fries. They are streamlined and graceful, with deeply forked tails and pointed heads. Even their olive- or steel-gray-and-white color seems classier than the bullheads' mud brown and frog-throat yellow. And perhaps because stronger muscles are needed to fight the current, their flesh is firmer and finer than that of their peasant relatives. In fact, to the unbiased eye a channel cat is more graceful than any bass that ever lived, and, in shape, except for its broad mouth and rolling eyes, not dissimilar to (I have to say) a trout.

You can fish for channel cats in much the same manner as for trout. If you follow certain iron-hard dirt roads off Highway 180 in the Gila until you reach the upright bars that mark the edge of the de jure wilderness, you can hike down into a landscape that, from above, looks about as hospitable as the moon. The climb down will make your joints creak, your knees ache, and your calves vibrate like plucked guitar strings. In the summer, it's also hot enough that you should probably start at dawn, or at that precise point in the afternoon when the sun is low but not so low that you'll have to hike past rattlers in the dark.

At the bottom, though, despite the heat reflected from rock to rock, it's a different world. The Gila sings over head-size rocks and seethes through pebbly runs. Clusters of walnut trees blossom in the angle between the wall and the river, a tropical green so vivid that they look almost poisonous. Some trail veils of wild grapes. Their shade is precise and almost cold. Golden Scott's orioles and luminous tanagers flash on and off like Christmas lights in the branches, and dozens of small unidentifiable flycatchers make short flights over the river and return, again and again, repetitious as skipping records.

Here is a good place to ease your transition from the Northeast to the Tropics. The setting is alien, but the water itself is almost familiar. If you go far enough upstream, you can even find trout; first stocked browns, then stocked rainbows, and finally, if you are persistent enough to backpack in, native goldens. This stretch, however, has no trout, but contains a healthy population of smallmouth bass. Cast your spinner or a streamer fly and that flash in the riffle is likely to be the same fish that attacks the same pattern on the Saco in Maine. Except when it has whiskers.

There is at least one more species of catfish in the rivers: the huge, ugly, voracious flathead, *Pylodictis olivaris*. It is narrow tailed and broad headed, mottled brown in color, and can weigh a hundred pounds. I have never caught one.

The flathead bears a close resemblance to the legendary European catfish or wels, *Silurus glanis*, which grows to fifteen feet. English writer and scientist Stephen Downes says of the wels, "There are various popular European stories, too, of the wels' feats: of the Hungarian angler who ran for three miles upstream by the treeless banks of the Danube with a giant wels in play; of the German wildfowlers who, instead of claiming to have seen wildfowl snatched under by giant pike, report the loss of their retreivers; Slavonic claims of child-eaters, man-eaters, horse-eaters . . . I repeat, they grow to fifteen feet."

Both the flathead and the wels are predators. You don't just dump any old inanimate bait in the river to catch them—they like their meals to be alive. You can use worms, but a fish of a size you wouldn't necessarily throw back is better. Best of all is the waterdog, a colloquial name for the neotenic or permanently larval stage of the tiger salamander.

You get these things out of stock tanks, and catching them is a minor hunt in itself. I recommend taking along an eager child like my friend Floyd's thirteen-year-old son, Brandon—their reflexes are quicker and they don't mind getting soaked. I finally managed to grab one myself as it lazed above the weeds near the tank's surface. It was about ten inches long, soft and slimy and vibrating with cold life. Its face looked a lot like the face of a catfish, and its color was a mottled olive. It had hands and feet. I do not mention this lightly. Even though it evinces little pain when hooked through its gristly lips or membranous tail, a waterdog is just a little too much an "animal" for me to be entirely comfortable using it for bait.

Yet I did want to go monster fishing, and I wanted very much to do it right, to suspend a large, active, living creature above the bottom as the dark came on and the great nocturnal predators began to stir . . .

I have done just that. I have gone down in search of river monsters half a dozen times now, down in the flooded no-man's-land south of the Bosque del Apache and north of Elephant Butte Reservoir. This is a strange place, flat and low, overrun with the feathery alien growth of tamarisk. The desert looms up above. The only solid ground is ditch banks. They run with geometrical precision along acequias that vanish ahead in perspective points like railroad tracks and that provide the only clear lines of view. Little groups of black, semiwild cattle appear and disappear in the salt-cedar thickets. It is hot and sticky and smells like water and dead fish and perfumed blossoms all mixed together. When a fitful breeze passes, it rattles the leaves on the immense cottonwoods that still dominate the ditch banks. The birds are primitive — black cormorants, coots and gallinules, a tropical profusion of snowy egrets. As dusk closes down they begin to tune up, and the river sounds like every grade-B adventure movie you ever saw when you were a kid. The only thing missing is crocodiles.

■

I'm down at the very end of the ditch-bank road, where it runs out into the narrow north end of the reservoir. The sun is down, although the high-desert ridges across the river still glow. Mosquitoes are whining by often enough to make me glad I reek of repellent. There is a night heron squawking across the ditch and something moaning in the weeds. I sit beside a seven-foot bait-casting rod, rather like the popping rods they used to favor for tarpon off the Texas coast, a rod I picked up in an Albuquerque store after rejecting dozens of too-short bass rods. It is equipped with a broad bait-casting reel big enough for salt water and two-hundred-odd yards of twenty-five-pound-test monofilament over a bedding of braided line. The rod juts up from a nest of rocks. Occasionally, its tip bends a little from the exertions of the foot-long salamander that swims tethered in circles thirty feet out. I watch it like a hawk, waiting.

I have been coming down here for weeks. I have caught silver and olive channel cats in the river by day and big-scaled reticulated carp in the ditches and backwaters at dusk. I haven't yet found a flathead. But I know he's out there.

Seasons of the Angler (1988)

PART IV

One
Review

The Great Debate

Bloodties: Nature, Culture and the Hunt
By Ted Kerasote (New York: Random House, 1993), 277 pp.

A View to Death in the Morning: Hunting and Nature Through History
By Matt Cartmill (Cambridge, Massachusetts: Harvard University Press, 1993), 331 pp.

Songbirds, Truffles, and Wolves: An American Naturalist in Italy
By Gary Paul Nabhan (New York: Pantheon, 1993), 227 pp.

I think it was Jim Harrison who said that, in a debate between the NRA and proponents of gun control, he'd rather be in a rowboat. Although I am a longtime member of the NRA, I know what he means; I can think of nothing more mind-deadening than being in the presence of two debaters with their minds made up, who reiterate the same old arguments at the top of their voices while utterly ignoring or missing each other's points. I can think of many other contemporary dyads where the volume of the battle drowns out sense: pro-choice versus antiabortion, evolution versus creation and, of course, the one that concerns us here—hunting versus antihunting. And though I'd much rather be in the hills on the day I'm writing this, the books I'm going to discuss here make or have made enough of a contribution to the sadly necessary debate that you, as thinking hunters, should be aware of them.

If you are as tired as I am of the debate but care about its essence; if you would like to see—perhaps be able to present—some original (if subtle) arguments for hunting, the book to get is Ted Kerasote's *Bloodties*. Kerasote, who has written for *Sports Afield* for years, is not your usual hook-and-bullet writer. His philosophical leanings are Buddhist, and he hasn't always defended the hunt. As he says in his prologue, he is someone who "grew up hunting, who renounced its violence, who became a vegetarian and who eventually went back to hunting." As someone who has been, thoughtfully, on all sides of the question, his account has unusual authority.

If you're looking for pure ammunition for debate—or what the critic and novelist Joanna Russ once called "detachable opinions"—forget it. For the most part Kerasote tells tales and presents scenes, leaving readers to draw their own conclusions. His account is divided into three sections: "Food," about his months with subsistence hunters in Greenland; "Trophies," in which he accompanies a group of wealthy trophy hunters to Siberia; and "Webs," a year at his home near Jackson Hole, observing life's rhythms and culminating with his killing an elk.

The Greenland third may be the most original, the most amazing. Although he has some initial difficulties being accepted (a Native friend explained: "I trust you. But the other hunters, who haven't talked to Sven like Nicolai and Peter have, they think you are from Greenpeace. And Greenpeace we all hate."), Kerasote manages to spend several months with the people, learning their language, hunting seals and (unsuccessfully) polar bears. It's a strange and almost magical piece of total-immersion travel writing, and it make you envy his experience—not to mention his descriptive ability. On his first seal: "It was a male, about three feet long and covered with black rosettes, giving the impression of a jungle cat. . . . His fur was wet and his body pliant—in fact, it was hard to feel where muscle and bone began. Lying on the ice, and discounting his predatory face, he resembled nothing so much as a furred slug." They cut it up, feed the dogs, eat some liver and blubber raw ("*Mamaq!*"—"tasty!" says Kerasote), then cook the small intestine: "He took it outside and sliced it into three-inch pieces, which he piled on another slab of blubber. . . . Surprise! It tasted like squid dipped in wasabi sauce."

This, for Greenlanders and other "Eskimos," is life—hunting and food, concepts closer together than they are for us. As Kerasote says, perceptively explaining *why* the natives "hate Greenpeace": "The point was to have southerners understand that eating agricultural products and livestock wasn't an option in the Arctic . . . that Greenlanders couldn't live like Danes or Parisians or people in Miami. Even if one disregarded the fact that asking northern peoples to give up their traditional diets was another form of imperialism, where would northerners get the money to pay for a diet totally composed of such processed foods?" Or, as he later asks antihunting activist Wayne Pacelle (whom we will return to later), "At what latitude would you stop heckling people for wearing fur?"

The second part of the book, "Trophies," may be the most difficult for self-aware hunters to read. In it Kerasote travels to a newly opened part of Siberia with a bunch of . . . gentlemen . . . from Safari Club International (SCI) and watches them make a travesty of sportsmanship. The biggest tragedy is that these are by no means evil people—just utterly and absolutely clueless; unable to see their own abuses and evasions; incapable of examining their own consciences; endlessly self-righteous and pompous and smug; content that their position at the top of the *economic* food chain justifies anything they want to do. They damn everyday, working-class hunters as "killers," but justify having sheep hazed toward them with helicopters. One, who has done some genuine good in conservation, is later convicted of multiple counts of trafficking in endangered species. If there's a prohunting cliché that one of them doesn't spout at some point, it's not one I'm familiar with. (Kerasote says later, apropos of the "we're-killing-them-so-they-don't-starve" argument: "Elk have starved with grace and dignity for thousands of years, and don't need Florence Nightingales with rifles to sanitize their deaths." Yes!)

The third and culminating section, "Webs," is the most personal; in it Kerasote tries to come to terms with his own hunting, and goes "into the belly of the beast" for an encounter with some radical antis. His own year is minutely detailed, a year of one of those hunters who, as he says in his prologue, "can't be conveniently placed in [a] group, but who hunt because they believe that the practice makes them a more mindful member of their bioregion." And his portrait of the antis, especially the cheerfully fanatic Wayne Pacelle, is at least as hilarious as it is depressing; it is hard to believe that anyone, in any mainstream, would take the hard core seriously if the antis were as candid in the media as Pacelle was with Kerasote. A few examples of the wisdom of Wayne: He tells Kerasote that, personally, "I don't want to see another cat or dog born." And about Greenland (remember the "what latitude" question?), they have the following exchange:

Pacelle: "Why do they stay there?"

Kerasote: "What?"

Pacelle: "Why do the Greenlanders stay there? . . . It seems like such a barren place to live."

Muses Kerasote: "Of all the questions we've discussed, this one seems to have the most obvious answer. I say, 'It's their home.'"

Pacelle "shrugs" and goes back to his newspaper.

■

But I don't want to leave you with merely the debate. *Bloodties* would be good even if it was merely an account of Kerasote's physical and philosophical ramblings around Jackson, a book full of wonderful, eye-opening turns of word ("fossil fuel vegetarian") and quietly affirmed acceptance of the world as it is. "There is no balance sheet, only a continuous departure and unexpected arrival, the flow of intimacy waxing and waning like the moon."

◼

Tom McIntyre, a colleague of Kerasote's at *Sports Afield*, was the one who insisted I read Matt Cartmill's *A View to the Death* (the phrase is from the old foxhunting ballad "John Peel"). He feared it would be the next great tool of the antihunters. At the risk of being considered smug, I doubt it. For one thing, it's not half the book that Kerasote's is; it's a well-written academic treatise with little in it that's not abstract—more a work of literary criticism than a polemic. Second, although it purports to be about "hunting and nature through history," it is more—I am being a *bit* reductionist here—a history of the deer-hunting tradition in literature, from the Greeks through Bambi, with a digression into the "Killer Ape" hypothesis of Raymond Dart.

And although it's well written and unfanatical, Cartmill just doesn't know enough to do a really good job. He attacks and burns down straw men. Surely no one today (except, maybe, certain SCI members!) really believes that Ardreyan killer australopithecines were our direct ancestors. Cartmill has a lot of fun with the darker tangles inside the heads of Hemingway, James Dickey, and T. H. White (and even takes a swing at McIntyre). But what has this to do with the universal human experience of taking life to feed life, of hunting species that are not big game, of the not-at-all-distinct boundaries between hunting and so-called "gathering"? Not all cultures define *the hunt* as "a confrontation between the human world and the wild." Current scholarship seems to indicate that, though organized hunting of what we would now call big game (or charismatic megafauna) only evolved in certain cultures, virtually all cultures ate some sort of animal protein.

It's all hunting, whenever we take an animal's life. One of the things that never ceases to amaze me is how little animal-rights activists know about animals. Toward the end of this book, Cartmill makes the following amazing statement: "Scientists are compelled to recognize those relatives [animals] as being in effect deformed human beings, differing from us only in certain genetic rearrangements that make them grow up funny-looking and stupid."

Or, as McIntyre puts it: "The [expletive] thinks that animals are deformed, funny-looking, and stupid!!!"

■

The debate will not be decided, of course, by hunters; in an urban society, we are too few. What will decide it is the fact that, when they are being honest, the animal rightists are fanatics who, like the ornithologist Robert Skutch, believe that God and/or evolution got the universe wrong, that it would run much better if some sensitive urbanite or Yankee professor could just redesign it. Such puritans are striving to attain a perfection that would be impossible to achieve even in an utterly totalitarian society.

Which is why a certain book, by a gentle, nonhunting naturalist, the ethnobotanist Gary Paul Nabhan, gives me hope. Nabhan walked through Italy on a pilgrimage to Saint Francis of Assisi's shrine. Although he didn't particularly sympathize with bird hunters on the holy mountain, he finally got a bellyful of militant vegetarian rhetoric. A Hare Krishna is making a speech at the Saint Francis fiesta: "Francis is to Italy what Ghandi is to India. He would not eat flesh. He lived off vegetables. St. Francis felt that animals were like us—his brothers—and that the world would be a better place *if animals did not kill each other.*" (Italics mine.)

Nabhan replies: "To me, this sounded like a message from those who would tame wolves, turn them into vegetarians, and change their remaining wild habitats into 'better places,' perhaps soybean fields and tofu factories. I had read oodles of text on St. Francis, and had never run across any that demonstrated Francis to be a pure vegetarian. Nor had I come across anything that suggested herbivory as the only way for all of the animal kingdom.

"Why is it more natural or spiritual to crush plant tissue against our molars than it is to rip animal tissue with our incisors?

". . . I could hear ringing through my ears the words that my Alaskan friend Richard Nelson had said. . . . 'All of us live by ingesting the lives of others. We can do this with respect for the plant or animal that will die so that we can live, or we can do it mindlessly.'

"If you cannot find terrain magnificent enough to take your breath away, gravitate to places that at least increase your heartbeat. Find land fit for the raccoons, foxes, or hares, and if the animal numbers eventually recover, for the occasional hunter to wander through without causing worry—country where you are satisfied with your encounters with other creatures, whether you hunt them or not."

Shooting Sportsman (1994)

PART V

Three Books I Love, and Why

T. H. White's *The Goshawk*

The Goshawk is a book about excruciatingly bad falconry. It is the best book on falconry, its feel, its emotions, and its flavor, ever written.

In 1936 Terence Hanbury White—always "Tim" to his friends—was between projects. He was thirty years old and had just left his job as the head of the English department at Stowe School to live in a primitive gamekeeper's cottage and write books.

He had some experience. He had written seven novels, all rather light and not too distinguishable today from many other period pieces, but well received. His last book was something different. He had been keeping diaries about his passions—fishing, hunting (on horseback after hounds, the only way English sportsmen allow the word to be used), "shooting" (birds), flying airplanes, and following "miscellaneous" pursuits. The book, *England Have My Bones*, was the first real T. H. White book, where the future creator of Merlin and Wart and Gos began to speak in his own distinctive voice. His biographer, Sylvia Townsend Warner, quotes him writing to a friend that his previous style was "constipated." But now he had been writing about things he loved, for his own amusement. An early reviewer, James Agate, paid this last book the right compliment, saying, "It is about subjects in which I am not even faintly interested. It is enchanting."

He was at that time the quintessential newly emancipated free-lance writer. He was not quite broke—the advance on *England Have My Bones* was good for the time, and the reviews were excellent. But he had expensive tastes, a Bentley convertible (which he had just totaled), salmon fishing, and shooting, and drinking. He was flamboyant, adventurous, often bombastic; also sensitive and, beneath the bluster, terrified. He was often depressed. His advance would not last forever. He "could not make my friends understand that I was working too."

White's stay at the tiny cottage—it had an outhouse, and a well rather than running water—has strange echoes of Thoreau and premonitions of the late 1960s. Like Thoreau—and like some back-to-the-landers many years later—he did not need to suffer. His cottage, while simple, was only a half mile from a road, and cost only five shillings a week. He went to the pub every night. The parallels with the sixties are even closer. War loomed on the horizon and White was in agony about whether it would be best to fight Hitler or to be a pacifist. He feared—as he would again in the nuclear fifties—the breakdown and end of civilization. He wanted to learn survival skills. He also was, in the words of a friend, a "dead serious writer" who wanted to write good books and live on them. As he wrote in a moment of despair to his old mentor L. J. Potts, "Writing books is a heartbreaking job. When I write a good one, it is too good for the public and I starve, when a bad one, you and Mary are rude about it."

It was in such a mood that he conceived of a very strange idea. In his wide reading on natural history he had encountered a nineteenth-century text on falconry. In it he read "a sentence which suddenly struck fire from my mind. The sentence was: 'She reverted to a feral state.' A longing came to my mind that I should be able to do this myself. The word 'feral' has a kind of magical potency which allied itself to two other words, 'ferocious' and 'free.' To revert to a feral state! I took a farm-labourer's cottage and wrote to Germany for a goshawk."

He didn't just want to train a hawk, though he certainly wanted to do that. A writer to the core, he meant to keep a diary and make it into a book. The truest proof of his dedication as both a writer and a falconer is that he never once stopped to ask if anyone wanted to read a modern book on the training of a goshawk.

He started his project in typical headlong White fashion. He was to write later: "I had never trained a serious hawk before, nor met a living falconer, nor seen a hawk that had been trained." He had three books: a "modern" one by Colonel Gilbert Blaine, mostly about peregrines, birds as different from goshawks as dogs are from cats; a nineteenth-century manual from Badminton Sporting Library; and a copy of Edmund Bert's 1619 treatise on *Hawks and Hawking*. (The last, incidentally, might have done him the most good had he not been constantly reading the books against each other and, worse, second guessing himself at every frightened, determined step.) But falconry is almost impossible to learn without a human mentor. White didn't have one, so he started alone.

Along with Gos, that is. White's friend David Garnett later compared *The Goshawk* to a seventeenth-century tale of seduction, or to *The Taming of the Shrew*. "Gos" is every bit as much a character (at one point White refers to him as "a person who is not human") as the narrator is. The very real story—which begins as comedy, approaches tragedy, and is reconciled in knowledge—is the tale of a bungled love affair.

The story unfolds in the past tense, but with a sense of the present so vivid that putting the book down is like waking from a dream. Disaster lurks around every corner. On his second day, Gos escapes in the barn with his leash attached. White knows enough from his reading to know he has made a big mistake; sure enough, the bird ends up hanging by his leash from a nail "head downward, in rage and terror." White adds ingenuously: "Why the leash had not then been tied to a perch, thus preventing his escape, I am not able to remember. Probably I had no perch, and anyway I was in the position of having to discover all these things by practice." Could it be his later, less defensive self who then comments, "It has never been easy to learn life from books"?

He makes the same kinds of mistakes throughout the whole affair. If Gos does well, he overfeeds him. He misjudges the bird's moods and appetite. He overcorrects him and lets him get too hungry. Once he hauls the still-leashed hawk down from a tree with a salmon rod, earning his righteous indignation.

Admissions like these drive smug old falconers to fury. They—I mean *we*—all made similar mistakes when we trained our first birds. White presents his earlier self as enthusiastic, furious, terrified, and ignorant, all at the same time. Reading *The Goshawk* can be like reliving a hopeless youthful love affair. You feel each mistake, each stupidity, each irrevocable slip just as if you performed it and could not call it back.

Such heartbreaking and hilarious self-recognition is hardly the only virtue of *The Goshawk*. The book also presents scenes of hallucinatory sleep-deprived beauty (White tries, like a seventeenth-century yeoman, to train the hawk by keeping both of them awake), learned digression, and mock-heroic humor, sometimes all in the same paragraph. Consider this paragraph, in which White tries to call Gos to him on the "creance," a fifty-yard-long line, to the tune of "My Lord Is My Shepherd"—and then, when he succeeds, all too typically blows it:

> I put Gos to the railing and retreated to a distance of forty yards, giving ten yards law in order to prevent his being checked in flight, and began to call and whistle. The pursed lips repeatedly proclaimed the Lord their Shepherd, urgently, caressingly, madly, nobly, slowly, rapidly, continuously, with

pauses: 'Dinner!' they blew, commandingly, pleadingly, majestically, rapaciously. 'Come along, Gos,' they panderingly, whiningly, peremptorily, softly articulated. 'Now, now,' they remonstrated, feeling rather thankful that this could be done without an audience, 'don't be silly, come-along, be-a-good Gos, Gossy-Gossy-Gos." And tiddly-tum, tiddly-tum, Tiddly Tum Tum repeated echo to whistle, whistle to echo.

For nearly ten minutes the extraordinary uproar went on the the still ridings. So far away that even his flaming eye could no longer be distinguished, the loved goshawk stood with his back to me, turning his head this way and that. At last he turned upon the perch, roused his feathers into a greedy puff, began to hop upon the railing. The pleas, the tuneless whistling, the staccato notes rose to an orgasm of lust for beef: in vain. They relapsed into the majestic, the quiet, the filled-with-silence pauses. Suddenly, after ten minutes during which he had cocked his head at the creance and visibly pondered its reliability as he moved about, suddenly, and without relation to the pathos of my music, sweet Gos began to fly.

To fly: the horrible aerial toad, the silent-feathered owl, the hump-backed aviating Richard III, he made toward me close to the ground. His wings beat with a measured purpose, the two eyes of his low-held head fixed me with a ghoulish concentration: but like headlamps, like the forward-fixed eyes of a rower through the air who knew his quay . . . Too frighteningly for words . . . too menacingly he flew, not toward the at-right-angles-held-out beef, but directly toward my face. At five paces nerve broke. I ducked, still holding the beef at the stretch of my arm, and stayed cowering for two beats of the heart.

Gos, of course, sweeps by and must be disentangled from a hedge, where White rewards him for not making a fuss. And so they proceed, from bumble through bungle to curse, weirdly interspersed with Zen-like moments of understanding and calm. ("As I put Gos to bed in the darkness, a new thought emerged. This time it was a quotation: To scorn delights and live laborious days. But it presented itself the other way about, saying: To live laborious days for their delight.")

The story of Gos ends in loss; White once again loses him with the leash attached and never sees him again. As Warner puts it, he "felt that book and livelihood were gone too," although he soon gets over the feeling and trains a second hawk, Cully, this time succeeding in part because he has learned what mistakes not to make.

He put the book aside. One reason was his embarrassment; one might have been his recognition that Gos's death seemed insignificant with World War II on the horizon. Besides, he was already at work on the book that was to make him famous: *The Sword in the Stone*, the first volume of *The Once and Future King*, which would contain a wonderful scene starring the mad goshawk Colonel Cully. From there he took his perpetually conflicted conscience to Ireland, where he would sit out the war. It wasn't until well after that, in 1949, when his publisher removed an uncomfortable lump from under a couch cushion and discovered the lost manuscript. He brought a copy back to London and wrote White that he wanted to publish it. White resisted, but the publisher asked Dave Garnett to read it and intercede. When Garnett loved it, White agreed, reluctantly. He wrote to this editor, "My shyness about it is personal. You see, apart from not wanting to spread one's personality naked before the public, I have become a much better falconer since then."

As Warner says, there were indications that his heart might get over it. He wrote a new coda with Cully's first successful hunt, and the book was published, to excellent reviews.

Since then, despite White's misgivings and the discomfort of unreflective falconers, it has wandered in and out of print, one of those books whose fans buy up dozens of copies to give to their friends. Some of its readers are hawk trainers with the insight to see themselves in

White, and to see the wisdom of his folly. After all, it was White, not some falconry guru, who realized the hard-earned irreducible core of falconry: "The thing about being associated with a hawk is that you cannot be slipshod about it." Others, readers of nature literature and seekers after serenity, might see that falconry was a metaphor for the difficulty and necessity of real relationships with nature, ". . . because the faculties exercised were those that throve among trees rather than houses, and because the whole thing was inexpressibly difficult."

I read T. H. White's *The Goshawk* and *The Sword in the Stone* years before I ever saw a gos. Thirty-some years later, I have a goshawk in the yard (her name is Sara, she is five years past the tough times, and she comes from the Wind River Range rather than Germany, but her nature is the same as that of Gos) as well as first editions of White's books on my shelf. I still reread *The Goshawk* every year. I don't read it because I am a falconer, or even a goshawker, but because it is one of the best books ever written about a human and an animal, and because it is as fresh and contemporary as though it had been written yesterday.

T. H. White's *The Goshawk* (1996)

Rob Schultheis's
The Hidden West

Every year in June I go to a small college in a northern Vermont town to teach a small course in nature writing. Founded almost ten years ago by the novelist E. Annie Proulx, Wildbranch Writing Workshop has been dedicated from the first to the idea that nature writing, outdoor writing—writing "with trees in it," to use the phrase of the editor who first rejected A *River Runs Through It*—is not a minor subgenre but a stream of literature with subjects and attitudes that are vital, even essential, to a healthy understanding of our world.

In our first year Annie may have known what she was doing, but I did not. I was a fairly well-established writer, but I lacked a degree and had never attended, never mind taught, a writers' workshop. I thought my background was erratic, to say the least. I had almost become a biologist, but then I switched to writing; I was a poor eastern ethnic kid with a fancy New England almost-education who had lived for more than ten years in a back-country dirt-road western town with neighbors of Spanish, Indian, and ranch descent. My only qualification was, to misquote Tom McGuane, that I had read like a son-of-a-bitch. I had read everything from classic novels to field guides, and I believed John Updike's elegant borrowing—that a writer was a reader moved to emulation.

These principles, and my attachment to the land of the West, became my tools for teaching. From my first terrified days, when I talked incessantly while fearing I had nothing to say, I heard myself saying three things: that writers had to read; that their love of reading had made them want to write; and that *nature* writing was a broad category with only one necessary component—it had to be rooted, deeply, in real places where humans come into intimate contact with the land. Nature books had to have trees (cacti, bears, hawks, the wind, sandstone, buttes, rain forests, buffalo bones, algae, horses, "how the weather was") in them.

As my fear of teaching receded, I found I held some strong intuitive beliefs about what good nature writing brought to literature. Too often the genre was legitimately dismissed by serious writers as either mere polemics or, worse, vaporous internal monologues on what nature means to *me* (emphasis on "me"), the kind of stuff often lumped under the awful neologism "journaling." To claim that nature writing is somewhat "spiritual" when it doesn't move the spirit of the reader seems to me a kind of self-indulgent arrogance.

I suspected that there might be another path entirely for writing about the natural world, one that could enrich all literature. The ideal nature writing could be descriptive or narrative, about or agonized by hunting, a travel book, even a book of intimate revelations about ants. But it would embody its ideas in things, in true observations of the real, in intimate, gritty knowledge. Its best practitioners would know animals, plants, rocks; their smells, sounds, tastes, and feel: Hemingway's "weather." These authors would know history, and not be content with only their personal reactions. If the writer knew and lived all these principles, he could write polemic or scientific material, comedy, or poetry; all would succeed in moving the reader; all would help us in our endless task of reconciliation with the world. Such ideas may seem primitive, but they remain the base of all effective writing.

I learned from Annie to push my students to write in class, not just in their off time; to handle short assignments with vivid writing, evoking their favorite landscapes, putting real animals and people into them. I searched for writers and passages that would inspire emulation. I introduced my students to essays by Annie Dillard, descriptions of tarpon fishing by Tom McGuane, poems by Ted Hughes. And I brought them passages from Rob Schultheis's *The Hidden West.*

On the first day of class I now read them the passage that begins, "If the mysteries of the Great Plains have a heartland, it is the Sand Hills of Nebraska." Schultheis introduces the area with a disconcerting image (one with a structure I suspect he stole from Churchill)— the grassy hills are a desert, a hidden one, with more secrets hidden inside them: "A sea inside a desert wrapped in green prairie." He brings you, the reader, into the scene in an intimate, active way, with vivid language that owes nothing to the piling up of descriptive words that students often think characterizes "fine" writing: ". . . dig. Beneath the brittle grass and the thin smoke of soil you hit sand: you are standing in a sea of dunes."

After setting the scene, he gives us a character, Martha Schaller, who was born there of a settler family. I don't know what kind of a person the reader would first imagine, but Martha "was six feet tall and weighed about a hundred pounds, still wore the Levi jacket she had gotten for her thirteenth birthday, smoked little black cigars and had been a model in Paris. Her childhood had been a honky-tonk fairy tale." He sets her family in the ghost-ridden landscape:

> Once as she rode home at winter dusk in a swirling Great Plains blizzard, her horse spooked and she looked up and saw (she said) an enormous white wolf, three feet high at the shoulder, leap the barbed-wire fence and race away across the white prairie. There was also an eroded sandstone bluff back

in the hills, and when you crawled in with a flashlight you found yourself in a vault that went as high as fifty feet in places. And there were bats: tens of thousands of the ruby-eyed little leather devils hanging upside down.

The "story," all of three pages long, ends in tragedy. Martha's father and his pal blow up the bat cave in a spasm of unnecessary fear of rabies. The Ogallala Aquifer, the hidden sea, begins to dry up. Martha returns to find her father drunk at his desk.

It's all over, he told her. Sand Hill's cattle ranching's dead. We've got maybe thirty years left, and then the whole business is going to dry up and blow away; from Denver to the hundredth meridian, this country's gonna look like Afghanistan. The dirt farmer and the rancher's gonna be as fifty million buffalo, as dead as Crazy Horse, as rare as a set of jackalope antlers. Ed Weicker and I and every other rancher in this country should have crawled in that cave with the goddamn bats and dynamited the door down from the inside.

I look at my students, as hushed and moved by this set of characters in a landscape, this piece of nature writing, as by any short story or tragic play. And I say, "Go thou and do likewise: Write me a piece of landscape that means that much to you. You have ten minutes." And I walk out the door.

I'm not surprised that I haven't quite gotten a *Hidden West* out of my students. But what I do get is consistently amazing, even to its writers. Schultheis suddenly gives them a chunk of landscape, with its biology and blood history, its enigmas and real, hard people; landscape "with the hair on," as Ed Abbey liked to say. It challenges my students to emulation because it is as fine in all ways as nature writing — *as writing* — can be.

The Hidden West came out in 1982 when I was a new westerner myself. It became a guidebook of sorts into a West that was neither overpromoted scenery nor romantically pristine Eden. Schultheis's West was full of rocks and ghosts, animals and stories and strange people. Schultheis didn't sing about Yellowstone or Santa Fe; his tales were of back country, the harsh badlands that tourists never even heard about. He knew of the Sand Hills of Nebraska, deep canyons that drain off the Colorado Plateau into the San Juan River, Aldo Leopold's lost Colorado Delta, the Taramuhara's Copper Canyon. He knew that the real places, where you can approach the mysteries of a region or have a profane conversation with its inhabitants, are more often than not "hidden." Schultheis knew his science and history and did not give into facile, neo–Native American mysticism. He had a hard-rock sense of humor. And yet, although he told stories that would make you laugh, he also knew ones that would make the hairs on the back of your neck stand on end.

Maybe another example would help. Schultheis is describing Dinetah, the Navajo country:

> The first time I went down to the Navajo reservation, driving south from Cortez, Colorado, the country struck me with the force of a foreign land: Mongolia during the reign of the Khans or nineteenth-century Afghanistan, perhaps. The men looked like Central Asian cowboys (later, in Tibetan refugee camps in India, I would see the same faces): flat, cuprous, epicanthic faces, many with long hair topped by incongruous felt Stetsons. . . . Driving south to Shiprock and west to Kayenta that first day on the reservation, I found I had entered a whole other cognitive universe; everything was different. Vast deserts of sage swept away to distant surreal mountains. An old Buddha-faced man walked away across the dunes, driving a herd of goats before him. Turquoise pickup trucks rolled down endless highways. . . . In a café near Teec Nos Pos I ate something called a Navajo taco: ground beef, chili sauce, onions and cheese, on a heavy slab of Navajo fry bread. The café was full

of big Indians in tall twenty-gallon hats. Two girls came in and ordered coffee. They began to talk in Navajo, a language that manages to sound both slurred and bitten off at the same time. Every once in a while, an English word would pop up in the soft stream of Athabascan: "basketball game," "Chevy pickup," "cheeseburger." One of the girls went over to the jukebox, put in a quarter and punched three songs: "Okie from Muskogee," "Purple Haze," and "Wasted Days and Wasted Nights" by Freddy Fender. Later that afternoon I picked up a hitchhiker, a kid on his way home to Kayenta: "My cousins and I started a rock-and-roll band," he told me. "We were doing great till Marvin got scared by witches and got sick."

Rob Schultheis has gone on to write good books on sports and the human body and the war in Afghanistan. *The Hidden West* has its cult readers and rabid fans (among them more than a few of my students), but it doesn't have the readership it deserves. Only a few authors get as close as Schultheis does to the flesh and bones of the Southwest—Chuck Bowden, Tony Hillerman, Leslie Silko, maybe sometimes Ron Querry; on different subjects, Gary Nabhan and James Corbett, Ed Abbey and Aldo Leopold. He's *that* good.

Maybe on some cosmic scale it's just as well that thousands of fans of *The Hidden West* have not descended on its fragile landscapes. But then those who love this book recognize one thing that it demonstrated: that everyone finds his hidden West.

Rob Schultheis's *The Hidden West* (1996)

Gavin Maxwell's
Harpoon Venture

I f you say the name "Gavin Maxwell" to any reasonably literate reader, he will be likely to respond, *"Ring of Bright Water."* In 1961, this
love letter to the wild west coast of Scotland and the otters—I can't
really call them "pets"—who lived with him there became an unlikely best-seller, making its author famous overnight. *Ring* is a wonderful book, like most of Maxwell's a bit hard to classify in any genre.
Nowadays Maxwell's books are usually considered "travel literature."
But *Ring*, his fifth, wasn't, nor was this one, his first and still one of
his best.

Gavin Maxwell was born in 1914 to an aristocratic family that
combined high birth, puritan rigor, and intellectual achievement. In
his youth he was interested in natural history and not much else. At
Oxford his major was in "Estate Management." He wrote and painted, went on an ornithological expedition to northern Finland, and
went off to war. Although he became a major in the Special Forces he
spent much of the war, as he was to spend a good deal of his life, as an
invalid. After the war a lifelong romantic fascination with the rugged
coast of Highland Scotland, still one of the world's "wilder places,"

drew him there in his thirty-foot lobster boat. He was thirty-one years old and looking for something to do.

He hit on an idea that, even after he explains it, can still amaze the reader with its crazed impracticality: He would outfit a fishing boat with harpoons and build a commercial fishery for the basking shark on the Isle of Soay (which he bought) in order to bring a useful industry to the depressed western Highlands. The plan was typically Maxwellian in that it combined romance, adventure, and danger with contact with nature and an impulse to do good. It was also typical in that it cost an enormous amount, that all financial signals pointed to disaster, and that he leaped into it without really looking to see where he was leaping. Or as he put it, always honest in hindsight: "When in November, I found myself a civilian I had finally made up my mind to experiment in commercial shark fishing. I had gone further than that: I had taken the first false step and bought a worthless and entirely unsuitable boat." As Mark Cocker would write in *Loneliness and Time*, his excellent book on English travel writers, "It was . . . inevitably a book about failure."

But what a book, and what a failure! All Maxwell's books are in part essays in autobiography, and despite their diverse subjects—the fishermen and bandits of Sicily, the now-vanished Marsh Arab culture of Iraq, otters, the brigand-lords of the Atlas Mountains, basking sharks and harpoons—his character remains as interesting as his interests. On the face of it, he is an unlikely macho hero, modest, introverted, sensitive, and impractical. He was often ill and suffered from (to use one list only) "synovitis of the right ankle, a duodenal ulcer and an enlarged heart." He had constant trouble with his circulation, which nearly crippled him in the sixties, and would die of lung cancer at fifty-five, perhaps because he habitually smoked eighty cigarettes a day.

On the other hand, he was a crack shot with rifle and shotgun, had a genius for taming wild animals, was utterly intrepid, and was a stoic in pain and disaster. Crocker characterizes him as "soldier, poet, journalist, portrait painter, conservationist, fisherman, writer. . . ." Perhaps an even better glimpse of his character can be seen in his choice of books for the shelf on his harpoon boat *Sea Leopard:* Is this the library of an Oxford aesthete, a man of action, or a biologist? "Eliot's *East Coker* was, I remember, stained by the damp green kiss of its green-covered neighbor, *Le Tannage des Peaux des Animaux Marins;* [poet Ray Campbell's] *Adamastor* rubbed shoulders with its avowed enemies, [critic Cyril Connolly's] *The Condemned Playground* and *Enemies of Promise,* and next to them came Hogben's *Principles of Animal Biology,* Empson's *Seven Types of Ambiguity,* Huxley's *Evolution,* and *A History of The Whale Fisheries.* Technical works on ballistics and navigation alternated with tattered novels, of which Evelyn Waugh claimed seven out of twenty. . . ."

Maxwell was a spendthrift who would live for years in a cottage with no modern amenities, a bisexual who married, a man who could cry for an otter or a dog but who hated the not-yet-romanticized killer whale. He had a love affair with the poet Kathleen Raine and used a line from one of her poems as the title of his most popular book, though this sometime man of science also believed that her curse had led to the death of the otter hero of the same book. "Contradictory" seems an inadequate word for him.

He adventured through the islands for three years. The "work" was always exciting, but the shoreside part of the business refused to go smoothly. It took an incredible amount of time and money to design a reliable harpoon head, partly because Maxwell had an idea about how to design one that he would not let go, despite the fact it never worked. (He was still fiddling with new harpoon and gun designs when the whole concern was bankrupt.) His first boat, as mentioned, was useless. A plan for pickling shark flesh went awry; they didn't use enough salt and ended up with sixteen tons of rotting flesh. "It was alive, heaving, seething, an obscene sea such as Brueghel might have conceived, alive as the sanctuary of Beelzebub himself, with a million

million grubs, twisting, turning, writhing, as though beneath that surface layer were the struggling bodies of all the wounded but resurrected dragons that we had attacked and that had escaped us."

They were only a little better at chasing his "dragons":

> I was able to fire into him at almost point-blank range, the gun at maximum depression, and the gigantic expanse of his flank practically stationary below me. I had loaded with a slightly increased charge of powder, and I could feel the decks below me shudder with the recoil as the harpoon went squarely home. The shark reacted very quickly, tipping to dive almost in the same instant as the harpoon struck, and the tail rising level with the *Sea Leopard*'s decks in a tremendous flourish. The tail was on a par with the rest of him; it seemed half as big again as any that I had seen. An average tail is about seven feet across; this looked to me like ten at least, and I bounded back from the gun as the flat of the tail slammed wetly on to the boat's side a foot below the gunwale. Then the shark was down under the water and the rope streaking out from the fairlead at tremendous speed.
>
> I stared, incredulously, watching a thin trickle of smoke rising from the rope where it passed over the metal—the first time I had ever seen a rope running out fast enough to be practically catching fire. I was aware of Dan behind me, trying hopelessly to slow the rope enough to catch a half-turn on the winch, but the speed was too great for him to do anything. It was a matter of seconds before the heavy thump of the rope snapping off short at the iron ring to which it was tied—a three-inch yacht manila rope with a breaking strain of about two tons.

He learned to fix this particular problem by attaching the rope to a buoy rather than to a fixed point, a method I saw used in the New England tuna fleet in the late seventies. But the problems multiplied even as the money dwindled and the pickled flesh rotted. The *Sea Leopard* turned out to be riddled with dry rot. Another ship ordered as a replacement was wrecked on a rock, and by 1950 the Soay Island Shark Fishery, a venture of "almost unlimited derring-do" according to a contemporary newspaper report, was no more. But Maxwell had observed well, kept a diary and notes, and in 1951 published his history of failure in a critically acclaimed book. It was not the last time he did that.

Today it seems almost no one has read it; I'm not sure why. Perhaps it's the cover, the title (the English edition, *Harpoon at a Venture*, reads as vaguely less aggressive), the dust jacket copy. Are modern readers wary of explicit adventure, equating it with cheap machismo? Are they too sophisticated for sea stories? The deserved success of the Patrick O'Brian stories would seem to argue against both points, though maybe their setting in the remote Napoleonic wars absolves them.

To me, *Harpoon* has a lasting appeal that is as complex as Maxwell's character. First, there's the sea; *Harpoon Venture* is one of the few great *modern* sea tales. I'll admit I'm an addict; I was born within smelling distance of the ocean to a mother whose people were maritimers back into the mists of time. Though I live in arid regions today, I don't need even that smell to arouse painful nostalgia, just a few well-chosen words. But again, judging from the sales of O'Brian's saga, you don't need salty blood or an oceanside upbringing to feel that yearning.

There is the problem of the shark fishery itself—how would *you* go about inventing an industry? There is science, plenty of it, for the rationalist and the biologically minded naturalist. Despite Maxwell's often-professed dismissal of "machinery," there is enough (fascinating) material on the evolution of his harpoons to satisfy an engineer. (He always admired and owned boats, expensive fast cars, and fine guns.)

And then you have the sheer grace of his writing, his powers of observation. So often he will turn from his problems and observe passing beauty with the delicacy of a Buddhist poet: "A single gannet was fishing in the Sound of Soay; he rose in a spiral, snow-white against the dark sea cliffs, and descended arrow-like, vertically, to strike a small splash from the surface of royal-blue glass." Sometimes he mixes the lyrical and the mechanical; here's a description of fulmars: "Beside them in the air the gulls looked clumsy and inept, old-fashioned laundaulettes beside modern racing cars, their flight lacking grace and style by comparison. . . . If there is enough breeze to make it possible, the fulmar takes off as does an airplane, with a short taxiing run on stiff outstretched wings that do not flap."

And sometimes all his skills come together in a perfect set piece, another kind of poem, like this miniature tragedy with its smaller dragons:

> Everywhere were little dragonflies of a bright electric blue; they darted low over the surface of the water, soared and remained momentarily stationary, alighted gem-like and delicately poised upon the smooth jade-green of the water-lily leaves. One pair, joined in that brief embrace of the insect world which seems so pathetically improbable, alighted near me; there was a whirring rattle of wings, and they were swept away by a huge yellow-banded dragonfly. He circled me, carrying the struggling pair, and alighted upon a lily close by. He did not finish his meal, but flew away, leaving them dead but still joined, a spot of colour suddenly robbed of meaning.

■

Maxwell lost all his money in his "harpoon venture." He would go through his life restless and reckless, usually poor, living beyond his means, writing down his experiences as fast as he lived them to stay afloat. Once, uncharacteristically, he complained: "I work for increasingly long hours every day, working simultaneously on *The House of Elrig* and *Lords of the Atlas*, but with an ever growing sense of frustration—and, I believe, a growing petulance and ill temper . . . I felt like an aphis, immobile and solicitously kept alive in a cell by ants who tended me assiduously for my daily excretion of written words." It's a feeling most writers know but, as I said, it was not typical. Despite all his disasters, I think he was a happy man, more so than most. He had the trick of looking at things sidelong—"Everything askance, and it all shines on," as Thomas McGuane said in *Ninety-Two in the Shade*. Maxwell turned his disasters into fine books, maybe art, even humor.

Gavin Maxwell's *Harpoon Venture* (1996)

PART VI

Food
and Life

Rissott': A Letter to John Thorne

When I saw the title of the autumn 1995 feature essay on risotto, "Desperately Resisting Risotto," I'm afraid that my reaction to it was the same as yours when you were confronted by the fuss surrounding risotto alla Milanese: instinctive aversion.

So much so that, for the first time since I started reading *Simple Cooking*, I didn't get beyond the first few paragraphs — at least not right then.

The reason was simple. My grandparents were Alpine Italians (from the village of Ispra on the east shore of Lake Maggiore, near Switzerland). I suppose you could call them peasants, although most Bodios worked in stone quarries. They emigrated in the early years of this century, and they kept an almost-farm, first in Boston and later in an inner suburb, until the early seventies. (They were both then pushing ninety.) They raised pigeons and rabbits, planted a small orchard and a huge garden, cultivated grapes, poached the occasional songbird, and even made their own wines (a harsh, dry red; odd ones from flowers). They dug dandelions and mushrooms.

They taught me what food was: Without them I wouldn't be a reader of *Simple Cooking*. (My late partner, Betsy Huntington, used to say that to love food you had to be exposed to both very good and very bad food when you were young, which I believe . . . but that's a whole essay, not a letter.)

Anyway, the important part here is: Risott' was a—possibly *the*— staple of their lives, second only to—maybe—their vegetables and bread and red wine. They had it twice a week or more, in many combinations. The constraints were *red* wine (more about that in a minute) and Parmesan (need I say, despite their being far from rich, never pregrated).

I grew up eating it, took it with me when I left home at seventeen in the sixties, and have eaten it—twice a week?—ever since. I consider it easy, hassle-free, infinitely variable, and delicious. While I often use good stock, I've never been a snob about it. My father insists that saffron, pronounced "zaffrun" in the odd northern Italian dialect, was an ingredient on feast days, but I swear I never saw yellow risotto until I had it in the early eighties.

Around that time I became amused by risott's rising stock (sorry) as a trendy dish. Yuppies were making acid-white-wine versions of my favorite food, insisting on babying it, raising eyebrows if I left the stove for a minute. They frowned on red wine and pure butter (they always used olive oil, at least in addition). I shouldn't be unkind here: My metabolism, inherited from Alpine peasants, could keep my blood cholesterol low on an all-cheese diet. They looked askance at the amount of Parmesan I stirred in. And then exclaimed at the deliciousness of the result.

Time has mellowed me. I've learned about champagne and good white wines in summer risott's and about adding such oddments as green grapes in same. I've learned some methods that use no stock at all (rather than the smaller-than-usual amounts I've always preferred). I still put Parmesan on everything, including seafood—hell, they do that in nearby (to Italy) parts of Provence, too.

So when the next issue of *Simple Cooking* came, I read the letters and found myself approving. A whole bottle of Barolo? Why not? Better than all stock! After all, the dominant tastes and odors should be rice, wine, and cheese. As I read your replies I realized that I hadn't given the original article a fair read. I went back and was embarrassed—but pleased—to find we agreed.

So a few more nonsnobbish tips from a lifetime of risott' eating. (I'll continue to drop the "o" to distinguish my staple from restaurant risotto.) First: Italian rices make great risott', but ordinary *medium*-grain rices produce enough starch to make a fine risott', and most supermarkets have them, even in country areas of New Mexico and Montana where I live. (Actually, short-grain "sweet" Asian rice can be interesting, too.) The only rice you must avoid is the long-grain variety. What this produces isn't "sticky," it's bad soup.

Second: As you've discovered, leaving the rice in the butter longer, almost until it sticks to the pan, is better than pouring in the liquid too soon. And that liquid should be as much wine as water: half and half. Red wine is generally better than white; it gives the risott' that "classic" taste. The result should be rather pink.

Stock is fine, if you don't overdo it. I'm an inveterate bird hunter and raiser, and I love bird stocks. But don't let them dominate. Wine and cheese—remember? Good stock is not as pronounced in flavor as bouillon, though my grandmother sometimes did add it. Proves she was Italian, I guess.

Third: Ease up! You don't have to finick around with it every second; you just have to keep it from sticking. I don't own a nonstick pan and have always made it in cast-iron skillets. It doesn't stick unless I get called to the phone. But I'll converse or read while I make it. Stir it each time you add some liquid. *Shake* the pan—a trick I learned from the completely non-Italian food writer Rebecca Gray. You can let your attention wander a little—this isn't polenta. (The yuppification of *that* peasant staple, even humbler than risott', is another modern weirdness. I make it sometimes—never did fall in love with it. However, I do remember it vividly with songbird sauce . . .)

Fourth: When it's almost done, take it off the burner. Let a couple of spoonfuls of butter sit on top. Pour yourself some wine. Sip. *Then* go put at least half a cup of Parmesan in. Stir and stir, and serve with more Parmesan at the ready.

It stays hot for a while, and you'll burn your mouth if you're tempted to start too soon. Every northern Italian kid I know remembers making little troughs in it and pushing it up against the sides of the dish to thin and cool. They all loved it then; I suspect they all still do.

Simple Cooking (1996)

Private Reconciliation Chili

I once conceived of this recipe as a metaphor—always a dangerous writerly conceit. I got the original from a friend, a food writer, when I lived back East. Took it to the West in 1980, to a dirt-road town. Added local ingredients. Served it to cowboys, Navajos, Spanish people from town, who pronounced it good. Brought the real thing back East once or twice on a visit, making sure I used not only New Mexico chilis but also antelope. Returned, made it for myself, living alone. Got caught by a cowboy friend putting chocolate in it, and was accused of being a yuppie. Agreed, and continue to make it for close friends, sometimes on request.

My personal life and the new range wars both twine through this metaphor in more ways than I intend to tell you. (One old friend, a teacher, says I give the reader too much credit. I want to.) My pilgrimage here, to New Mexico's still (briefly?) unchic dry southwestern back country; my love of my new home, perhaps uncritical and romantic; my attempts to explain its virtues; a death, a departure, a return; the realization that I will never be a native; my decision to stop participating in wars whipped up by outside forces, governmental and economic and philosophical; my home, my *querencia*, my friends.

■

Here are the basic ingredients. The animating idea is "local." Theoretically, except for the spices, you can do a version of this almost anywhere, but you should change it.

Meat: a lot—a pound or more. Cut it into small chunks or short strips so it cooks easily. I prefer a lean base meat. The three best are elk, antelope, and *lean* (no feedlots) range beef. Deer is a decided second, oddly.

If you want some subtleties, mix in feral pig (south Texas)—I know it's not native, you're improving the range—or, best, a well-cleaned javelina.

Experiments with stranger things are encouraged but not sanctioned.

Fat: Best is pork back fat. Suet, pancetta, or blanched bacon will serve.

Chilis: at least one large or five small smoked dried chilis—anchos or chipotles—torn into pieces with your fingers, using everything but the stems. This is most important for the taste. Also, five dried pequins, torn up, for heat.

Chili powder: Use a tasty brand, but not the hottest, for flavor and color. I prefer Chimayo.

Spices: at least half a head of garlic. At least a tablespoon of cumin—the best way is to parch and pulverize in a mortar some whole seeds, for a drier taste. At least a tablespoon of oregano—best wild, harvested on the dry New Mexico plateaus in a year of good rain when the aftermath of a shower on the Rio Salado smells like a pizza shop, hung up to dry, and crumbled into a jar against the arid years.

Stock: I always make my own, but really any robust version will do. Hell, bouillon cubes will do—all the spices are going to dominate the taste anyway.

There should be salt—this is not health food, though I'll defend its healthfulness.

Chocolate: about half an ounce (or a little more, with more meat) of unsweetened baking chocolate.

Masa harina: Blend a full tablespoon with a similar amount of heated stock—necessary for the true taste.

Heat the stock. Smash and clean and chop the garlic. Toast the cumin. Shave the chocolate into thin curls.

Heat the fat in a cast-iron skillet, one with a cover, for later. Add the garlic and dry chilis, then the meat. Brown vigorously.

As the meat starts to lose the liquid it generated at first, add the cumin, oregano, and at least a tablespoonful of Chimayo chili powder. Turn and coat everything. Take a sip of your preferred beverage— Jack Daniels, Bud, Coors, Perrier, O'Doul's—and be patient. When everything looks crusty and smells wonderful and is sticking, pour in enough stock to cover. Bring to a boil.

Stir in the chocolate shavings and masa mixture. Reduce the heat to the lowest simmer. Cover.

Two hours, at least, should ensue. Taste constantly. Add liquid if you need to, but remember it should be both tender and almost sticking to the pan at the end.

Now your gathering should not be homogenous, unless it is your biological or chosen family. It should at a minimum contain a representative of a ranch family (minimum two generations on same land), a newcomer, an Earth First! type (I'd say a vegetarian but for the obvious impossibility), a bowhunter, and at least two genders. Preferably there should be a Native American (we can argue about terminology, but everyone understands my meaning) and, in the Southwest, someone of Spanish or Mexican descent.

You should have a reasonable amount of alcohol, and be able to argue and even pound tables without shooting anyone or walking out.

There should be no representatives of the government, major environmental organizations, or People for the West present, at least not in official capacity.

When the chili is ready, serve with potatoes, beans (not mixed in!), salad, sharp cheese, more beer, more whiskey, gold tequila, Gigondas, flour tortillas, Italian bread. *Stop the discussion.*

Finish off with a final shot, or water.

Go outside together. Look at the moon. Feel the chill, or smell the blossoms, or hear the frogs, or listen to the coyotes, Breathe. Shut up. Breathe.

Redneck Review (1994)

Meat

"How, given the canine teeth and close-set eyes that declare the human animal to be a predator, had we come up with the notion that oat bran is more natural to eat than chicken?"
— *Valerie Martin,* The Great Divorce

My life has been built around animals and books about them. They have been in every book I've written and most of my essays. I was imprinted on the *Jungle Book* and Peterson's *Field Guides* before I was four, fated to be a raving bibliophiliac as long as I lived. I fed myself a constant diet of books with animals—Darwin, Beebe, Lorenz on the one hand, Kipling, Seton, Terhune, Kjelgaard on the other. I read bird guides like novels and novels about pigeons. As long as I can remember I kept snakes, turtles, insects, pigeons, parrots, fish; bred them all, learned falconry and dog training, kept life lists, raced pigeons, hacked falcons for the Peregrine Fund, did rehab, joined conservation groups, supported veterinarians, partnered for life with bird dogs. I would say I "loved" animals but for the fact the word is so worn out in our culture that I distrust it. (Valerie Martin again: ". . . . a word that could mean anything, like love. At dinner last night Celia had said, 'I love pasta. I love, love, love pasta,' and then to her father who had cooked the pasta for her, 'And you Dad. I love, love, love you.'") Suffice it to say that some animals are persons to me as well as points of focus, subjects of art, objects of awe, or quarries.

And yet? I eat meat, and always will. Which today is not only becoming vaguely suspect in some civilized quarters but also might be one point of dissension with what I understand of Buddhism. Although I also take a quote from a modern Buddhist everywhere I wander about this subject—at a bookstore, Gary Snyder once grinned as I handed him my copy of *Turtle Island* to autograph, opened to the poem "One should not talk to a skilled hunter about what is forbidden by the Buddha."

I recently announced too loudly at a dinner that I would no longer write anything with the purpose of convincing anyone to do anything. If writing essays means anything to me it is as an act of celebration and inquiry, like, if lesser than, poetry and science. With that in mind, let this be an inquiry into meat and, as my late friend Betsy used to say of the Catron County Fair, "a celebration of meat." I will try to be honest, even if it means admitting to crimes. Maybe this is about love after all.

■

Personal history does shape us all. I was born to blue-collar stock in the postwar suburbs. My mother's people were Irish and Scottish and English and German. Some had been farmers, one a revolutionary, and many had been fishermen, but by the time of my birth they had escaped the land and become respectable, things my animal-obsessed intelligence rejected without analysis. McCabes tended to react with disgust to the messier parts of life. I still remember with delight my outspoken little sister Anita, who used to help me clean game, when she came to visit me with our grandmother and found me making a study skin from a roadkilled woodpecker. She was all of eleven at the time, when many little suburban girls think they must be fastidious, but she scooped up the carcass and tossed it in the waste-basket. "You'd better get that covered up," she giggled, "or Nana McCabe's gonna puke all over the kitchen floor."

But the Bodios, who came over from the Italian Alps in their and the century's late teens, were from another planet than the lace-curtain Irish. My father had a furious drive toward WASP respectability, but his folks were Italian peasants who happened to live in Boston. Less than ten miles from downtown, they maintained until the ends of their long lives what was almost a farm. I believe their Milton lot contained half an acre's space. On it they had twelve apple trees, grapevines, and a gigantic kitchen garden. They also kept a few pigeons and rabbits. (No chickens — even then, Americans objected to the happy noise that half the planet wakes up to.)

Nana McCabe could cook pastries and cakes, but the Bodios *ate*. Eggs and prosciutt' and Parmesan, young bitter dandelions and mushrooms picked almost anywhere, risott' and polenta that, when I was very young, would be garnished with a sauce I learned ("don't tell nobody") was made from *uccelini*, "little birds" — I suspect sparrows, bushwhacked in the pigeon house. Eels and mussels — which, back then, had to be gathered rather than bought. I tasted real vegetables there, not like the canned ones at home — tomatoes and corn eaten in the garden, warm from the sun, with a shaker of salt, zucchini and eggplant soaked in milk, breaded, and fried in butter like veal. Tart apples, stored in the cool cellar where Grandpa kept his homemade wine. That wine, served at every meal, to kids and adults alike.

And, of course, meat, interesting meat. My father hunted and fished and kept racing pigeons, but has always been indifferent to food. I suspect that, until his own old age, he found his parents' food too "ethnic," too reminiscent of the social barriers he wore himself out trying to transcend. As for my mother, she hated game — the mess of cleaning and its smells, the strangeness of its taste. She passed this down to most of the kids; my sister Wendy so abhorred the idea of venison that my brother and I would tell her steak and veal were "deer meat" so we could get her portion, a subterfuge so effective that she would leave the kitchen, claiming to be nauseated by the imagined smell.

So the good stuff often went to the Bodios by default. *Really* good stuff—black ducks with a slight rank taste of the sea, ruffed grouse better than any chicken, white-tailed deer that would hang swaying in the garage until the meat formed a dry crust and maybe a little mold. Bluefish, too rich ("fishy") for my mother's taste, and fifty-pound school tuna.

I don't know if my parents ever realized that I, tenderest minded and softest and most intellectual of their kids, was also the one being trained to the delight of strange food, strange meat, even if the eating of it conflicted with my other "principles." My father would snap a pigeon's neck without a thought if it was too slow in the races, but he wouldn't eat it. I would cry when he "culled" (never "killed") a bird, then eat it with delight at my grandparents'.

I thought then that I was weird, and felt guilty. Now I think it's my father who was weird, and my tender-minded sisters, who would be vegetarians if they had to kill their meat. They "love" animals, deplore my hunting. Only one of the six of them keeps animals, which are messy and take work to keep and know.

All these as-yet-unexamined attitudes and preferences came with me when I left home at seventeen. I became *seriously* weird at that point—to my parents, of course, because I grew my hair long and cultivated a beard and disagreed with them on sex, religion, politics, drugs, and money—but also, to my surprise, to many of my new friends. They of course shared my beliefs about all of the above. But at that time I usually lived in freezing shacks in seaside outer suburbs like Marshfield, with trained hawks and my dad's old .410 and 16-gauge shotguns, and "lived off the land" in a way rather unlike that of rural communards. I spend so much time in the salt marshes that one girlfriend called me, not without affection, "Swamp Wop."

I shot ducks and geese all fall, gathered mussels and quahogs and soft-shell clams. You could still free-dive for lobsters then without being assaulted by legions of vacationing boat thugs. Squid swarmed in the summer and would strand themselves in rock pools on the spring tides. In summer we—my uncivilized blue-collar workmates and I, not my friends who agreed with me on art and politics—would use eelskin rigs and heavy rods to probe for stripers in the Cape Cod Canal. Winter would find us on the sandbars, freezing but happy as we tried for a late-season sea duck for chowder or an early cod on a clam bait for the same.

Gradually I achieved some small notoriety—not just as some sort of nouveau primitive, but as a guy who could serve you some serious food. In the late seventies I was a staff writer for a weekly postcounterculture paper in Cambridge and began to introduce occasional animal and/or food pieces to its pages. We had entered the age of debate on these subjects, but I still had fun. Just before the paper died, the food writer Mark Zanger, who still writes under the nom-de-bouffe "Robert Nadeau," and I were going to do a game dinner extravaganza, to be titled "Bodio Kills It, Nadeau Cooks It," complete with appropriate wines and between-the-courses readings from my game diary. But the owners folded the paper and I left for New Mexico, a more hospitable ecosystem for my passions.

■

I present the above as a partial recounting of my bona fides, but also to present you a paradox. America and American civilization are still "new" compared to, say, France, Italy, China, Japan. The movement against meat and the "Animal Rights Movement" are largely a creation of American or at least Anglo-Saxon culture, which doesn't have the world's richest culinary tradition, to say the least.

My friends considered me a barbarian, yes, but also a cook.

France and Italy and China (and even Japan—fish, after all, is

meat, the "meatless" Fridays of my youth notwithstanding) eat *everything*. They eat frogs and snails, eels and little birds, dogs and cats (and
yes, deplorably, tigers and bears), snakes, whales, and poisonous puffer
fish. They actually eat less bulk of meat than our sentimental in-denial
culture of burger munchers, but they are in that sense more carnivorous—or omnivorous—than we are.

People who eat strange meat are considered "primitive" by our
culture, whether or not theirs has existed longer than ours, or created
better art and happier villages.

So are our oldest ancestors, hunter-gatherers, who eat thistles and
birds and eggs and grubs, roast large game animals and feast on berries
like the bears they fully realize are cousins under the skin. Hunter-
gatherers know animals are persons, and eat them.

Can it be that we are the strange ones? We, who use up more of
the world's resources than anyone, even as we deplore the redneck his
deer, the French peasant his *grive*?

Can it be entirely an accident that in the wilds of southern
France the wild boar thrives in the shadow of Roman ruins? That carefully worked-out legal seasons for thrushes exist alongside returning
populations of griffon vultures, lammergeiers, peregrines? That you
can eat songbirds in the restaurants and look up to see short-toed eagles
circling overhead? Just over the border, in Italy, they still have wolves,
while in wilderness-free England and Brussels, Euromarket bureaucrats try to force the French to stop eating songbirds.

■

Three years ago I spent a month in the little Vauclusien village
of Serignan-de-Comtat. Animals and books brought me there—in this
case, the insects and books of the great Provençal naturalist and writer
Jean-Henri Fabre.

The Fabre project didn't come off. But upper Provence finally
gave me a template, or maybe a catalyst, to crystallize my disconnect-

ed thoughts about nature, eating, wild things, and culture into a coherent form.

The thing is: I had expected insects, sure; stone medieval villages, good food, wine and vines, lavender and broom, Roman ruins and the signs of long occupancy of the land.

I hadn't expected anything like "the wild." But on my first walk into the dry oak hills behind the town I looked up into the brilliant yellow eyes of a hovering short-toed eagle, a *circaete de Jean-le-Blanc* bigger than an osprey, with the face of an owl and long dangling legs. The snake eater soon proved common, as did red kites, almost extinct in Great Britain. A week or so later I was hiking on the flanks of Mont Ventoux in a landscape that reminded me enormously of the Magdalenas at home when I saw a soaring hawk suspended over the deep valley between me and the next ridge. This one resolved in my binoculars into the extremely rare — but returning — Bonelli's eagle, a sort of giant goshawk.

More evidence of the paradox kept coming in through the month. Restaurants, like the Saint Hubert — it was named after the patron saint of hunters — sold boar and duck; the proprietor told me to come back in the fall and eat *grives*, "thrushes." A nature magazine discussed the reintroduction of griffon vultures west of the Rhône. Birders directed me to the bare stone teeth of the Dentelles, south of Ventoux, where the bone-breaking lammergeier or bearded vulture was nesting. I didn't think they existed any longer west of the Himalayas! I caught a jazz concert in the Théatre Antique, a Roman theater in Orange, in continuous use since before the time of Christ. I looked down from wild hills with sign of badgers and foxes and deer into the ordered lines of vineyards.

Then came the morning at dawn when I surprised the two middle-aged men in camo fatigues loading their two hounds into the back of a Deux Chevaux. They replied curtly to my cheery *"Bonjour,"* but I was fascinated. *"Je suis un chasseur Americain,"* I began: I'm an American hunter . . .

The transformation was instantaneous; they both shook my hand and began speaking over each other in quick French made even tougher to understand by their heavy local accents. "You're *American*, that's good. . . . We thought you were from Paris . . . those northerners, they think they're better than us. They don't hunt, they hate hunters . . . they are all moving down here to their summer houses." I felt like I was in New Mexico. Then I caught, "Did you see the boar, M'sieur?"

I must have looked skeptical, because they led me to its track in a mud puddle across the path. The soil hadn't even settled from the water; the great beast (its tracks were huge) must have crossed the path just seconds ahead of me.

They hung around to show me game waterers to allow the animals to drink during the dry summer months, to invite me to share a *pastis* at the bar in town, to ask me to return in the fall when we could eat truffles and partridge and *bartavelle* (a kind of chukar) and *grives* and boar. I realized that, unlike in England and Germany, *everybody* hunts in France — the butcher and baker and mechanic as well as the local personages. Maybe it's the French Revolution, maybe the Mediterranean influence. I doubt that the sign on the tank, posted by my new friends and their fellow members of the Serignan hunters' society, would have appeared in England or Germany or the United States: NATURE EST NOTRE CULTURE: "Nature is our culture, our garden."

Nature *is* our culture. Our "permaculture," if you will; something a part of us, that we're a part of. Nobody in rural southern France is ignorant of what food is, or meat.

I had been trying to live something like this for as long as I had been conscious. I hunted, and gathered, and gardened, and liked it all. I spent my rather late college years in rural western Massachusetts, put a deer in the freezer and cut cordwood, some of which I sold to professors. I ate roadkill for two years, cruised the roads at dawn for carcasses of cottontails and snowshoe hares and squirrels, praising whatever gods when I found a grouse (I barely had time to hunt except during deer week), learning you could cook snake and make it good. I even ate a roadkilled hawk once—it was delicious.

But the French visit gave me a more coherent vision. Having confessed to one crime (yes, roadkill picking is generally illegal), I'll tell you of a worse one. Or—no, let me tell this in the third person.

A naturalist recently returned from France awoke one fall morning to find his rowan trees full of hundreds of robins feeding on the red berries. He went to feed his goshawk and found the cupboard bare. But the season hadn't started.

He thought long—well, maybe five minutes—about France and food and his hungry hawk. Opened the window. The robins flew up, then returned to their gobbling.

Robins are true *grives*, "thrushes" of the genus *Turdus*. In the fall they grow fat on fruit.

He tiptoed to the gun room, got out an accurate German air rifle, cocked it, loaded it. Stood inside the open window, in the dark of the room. Put the bead on a fat cock's head and pressed the trigger. One thrush fell, the rest fled to the higher trees. He walked out, collected the fallen bird, admired its lovely colors, felt its fat breast. Made sure the pellet had passed through the head, took it to his gos's mews, where she leaped on it with greedy delight.

Now, though, he's *really* thinking. He gets down his copy of Angelo Pellegrini's *The Unprejudiced Palate* and reads, "People now and then complain that their cherries, raspberries, strawberries are entirely eaten by the birds. . . . When this is true, the offending songsters should be captured and eaten." Well, he hardly considers the robins to be "offending," but they certainly were eating fruit. Pellegrini adds that they are "delectable morsels unequaled by any domestic fowl or larger game bird." Hmmm . . .

He goes to his copy of Paul Bocuse, which features a dozen

recipes. He likes the one that adds sautéed potato balls and garlic to the briefly roasted whole thrushes.

He goes back to the window. Fires six times. Six times a bird falls; six times the others flee for a moment, then return to their feasting.

He plucks them, but leaves the head, feet, and innards. Roasts them in a 425-degree oven for ten minutes. Combines them with the potatoes and sautéed garlic. Shares them with his wife, a kindred spirit, accompanied by a red Italian wine.

He tells me that they were delicious and that he doesn't feel guilty at all.

∎

Delicious, of course. Food should be delicious, and inexpensive, and real; the last two keep it from being mannered or decadent. My hunting and gathering and husbandry are driven both by principle and by pleasure—why should they not be driven by both? But because the "good people" in our northern Protestant civilization-of-the-moment are so often gripped by a kind of puritanism even as their opposite numbers rape the world with greed (did I write "opposite"? I wonder . . .), most writers do not write of the sensuous pleasure of food. Okay, a few: M. F. K. Fisher, first and always; Patience Gray; Jim Harrison; John Thorne. But even they don't write enough about the pleasure of *meat*. So before we return full circle to principle, to guilt and remorse, to "why," let's take a moment to celebrate the delights of our subject.

If we weren't supposed to eat meat, why does it smell so good? Honest vegetarians I know admit they can be forced to drool by the sweet smell of roasting birds. No food known to humans smells quite as fine as any bird, skin rubbed with a clove of garlic, lightly coated with olive oil, salted, peppered, turning on a spit over a fire . . .

Why do we Anglo-Saxons overcook our meat? Another residue of puritanism, of fear of the body, of mess, of eating, of realizing that death feeds our lives? Do we feel that guilty about not photosynthesizing?

Nobody could tell me that wild duck tastes "of liver" if they cooked it in a five-hundred-degree oven for fifteen or twenty minutes.

No one could say that venison does, if they dropped thin steaks into a hot skillet, turned them over once, and removed them and ate them immediately.

Hell, nobody could tell me that *liver* tastes "like liver" if they did the same, in bacon fat, with onions already well cooked piled around it.

A cowboy I know used to say he hated "nasty old sheep." We changed his mind when we bought a well-grown lamb from the Navajos, killed and skinned and gutted it, and let it soak for a day in a marinade of garlic, honey, chilis, and soy sauce, turning it frequently. Then Omar and Christine, Magdalena's prime goat and lamb roasters, cooked the legs and ribs over an open fire, until a crust formed over the juicy interior. The smell could toll cars passing in the street into Omar's yard. Omar and I, especially, are known to stab whole racks of ribs off the grill with our knives and burn our mouths, moaning with pleasure.

Stock: I put all my bird carcasses in a big pasta pot with a perforated insert. I usually don't add vegetables. I cook them for ten to sixteen hours, never raising the stock to a boil . . . *never*. The result perfumes the house, causes shy friends to demand to stay for dinner, ends up as clear as a mountain stream but with a golden tint like butter. Then you can cook the risott' with it. But you only need a little—the real stuff uses more wine or even hot water, and a lot of Parmesan.

I love my pigeons, but have you ever eaten "real" squab, that is, five-week-old, fat, meltingly tender pigeon? I keep a few pairs of eating breeds for just that. You could cut it with a fork.

How about real turkey, the wild kind? It actually tastes like bird, not cardboard, and has juice that doesn't come from chemical "butter." Eat one, and you'll never go back.

How about the evillest meats of all, the salted kind? How about prosciutt', with its translucent grain and aftertaste like nuts? How about summer sausage? Old-style hams with a skin like the bark of an oak? How about real Italian *salame*, or capicolla?

Good things could be said about vegetables, too, by the way. We here at the Bodio household actually eat more vegetables than meat; meat is for essence and good gluttony, not for bulk. We eat pasta and rice and beans, cheese, good bread, garden vegetables by the ton, roasted vegetables, raw ones. But these things don't need a defender. Meat, improbably to me, does.

■

Let's veer in through that sensuousness once more. Last month I was preparing five domestic ducks for a feast with friends. To cook it the best way the breast meat had to be blood rare, the legs well done with a crispy skin. Which of course involved totally dismantling the ducks, hard work. You had to partly cook them, then skin them, getting seriously greasy. (The skin would become crackling, or as Libby called it, punning on the pork-crackling *chicharonnes* of New Mexico, "pata-ronnes.") You had to fillet the breast meat from the bone, and disjoint the legs. The carcasses had to go back into the oven for browning, and then into the stockpot. You ended up physically tired, sweaty, with aching hands, small cuts everywhere, and slime to your elbows. You felt good, accomplished, weary. But it was hard to avoid the idea that you had cut up an animal, or five.

Or take a *matanza*, a pig killing, in Magdalena. After shooting the pig in the head (if you do it right, the other pigs watch, but nobody, not even the hero of the feast, gets upset), it's work, work that will give you an appetite. The pig is carried out on a door, wrapped with burlap sacks boiled in one half of a fifty-gallon drum, scraped, hung up. It is eviscerated, and the viscera are washed and saved. The bulk of the "real" meat, all that will not be eaten that day, goes to the freezer. The *chicharonnes* are cut up and heaped into the other half of the drum, to sizzle themselves crispy in their own fat. Everything steams in the cold air—the fires and vats, your breath, the pig's innards. Those innards are quickly fried with green chilis and wrapped in fresh flour tortillas so hot they'll burn your tongue, to give you energy to rock that carcass around, to stir the *chicharonne* vat with a two-by-four. The blood is taken in and fried with raisins ("sweet blood") or chilis ("hot blood") and taken out to where you are working. By afternoon you are as hungry as you have ever been. You eat like a wolf. You also can't avoid the idea that you have taken a life. Afterward you all lie around like lions in the sun.

I once mentioned a *matanza* in a piece I wrote for the Albuquerque *Journal*. An indignant letter writer (from Massachusetts!) called me "refuse" for my "Hemingwayesque" love of "blood, hot and sweet," which he assumed was a grim metaphor rather than a rural delicacy. He hurt my feelings. But maybe he was right, in a way he hadn't intended.

So, okay, *death*. And cruelty.

Deliberate cruelty is inexcusable; I won't say much about it here. As I get older I actually use bigger calibers and gauges than when I was young; I can't stand wounding anything.

But death? We all cause it, every day. We can't not. Tom McGuane once said, "The blood is on your hands. It's inescapable." Vegetarians kill, too . . . do they seriously think that farming kills nothing? Or maybe they're like the Buddhist Sherpas that Libby used to guide with, who would ask her to kill their chickens and goats so the karma would be on *her* hands.

Let me pause for a moment to quote from two yet-unpublished books, books that might find publishers more easily did they not reject a lot of current foolishness. From Allen Jones's *A Quiet Violence*, a philosophical investigation of hunting: "The vegetarian does have good intentions. He or she is making an honest attempt to relate more directly to the natural world. The irony, of course, is that in denying their history they have placed themselves farther away from the process. . . . When death is seen as evil, or if pain is something to be rejected at all costs, then nature itself is in danger. If most animal rights activists had their utopias, neither ecology nor evolution would exist."

And from Mary Zeiss Stange's forthcoming *Woman the Hunter*: "Far from being a mark of moral failure, this [hunter's] absence of guilt feelings suggests a highly developed moral consciousness, in tune with the realities of the life-death-life process of the natural world."

An acceptance of all this is not always easy, even for the hunter and small farmer, who usually know animals far better than the vegetarian or "anti" or consumer. I find that as I get older, I am more and more reluctant to kill anything, though I still love to hunt for animals, to shoot, and to eat. Still, I am determined to affirm my being a part of the whole mystery, to take personal responsibility, to remind myself that death exists, that animals and plants die for me, that one day I'll die and become part of them. "Protestant" "objectifying" "northern" culture—I use those quotation marks because none of those concepts is totally fair or accurate, though they do mean something—seems to be constantly in the act of distancing itself from the real, which does exist—birth, eating, juicy sex, aging, dirt, smells, animality, and death. Such distancing ends in the philosophical idiocies of the ornithologist Robert Skutch, who believes sincerely that God and/or evolution got the universe wrong by allowing predation and that he, a Connecticut Yankee, would have done better.

I, on the other hand, don't feel I know enough about anything to dictate to the consciences of others. I certainly don't think that anyone *should* kill, so long as they realize they are no more moral than those who do; I can find it hard enough myself. While I suspect the culture would be saner if we all lived a bit more like peasants, grew some vegetables out of the dirt, killed our own pigeons and rabbits, ate "all of it" like bushmen or Provençal hunters or the Chinese, I have no illusions that this is going to happen tomorrow. I can only, in the

deepest sense, cultivate my garden, sing my songs of praise, and perfect my skills. I'll try to have what Ferenc Maté, calls "a reasonable
life," strive to be aware and compassionate and only intermittently
greedy, to eat as well as my ancestors, to cook well and eat well as a discipline and a joy. The French say of a man who has lived well that "*Il
bouffe bien, il boit bien, il baise bien*": "He eats well, he drinks well, he
[in this context] fucks well." Sounds like a life to me.

And in living my good and reasonable life, I suspect I should
sometimes kill some beautiful animal and eat it, to remind myself what
I am: a fragile animal, on a fierce fragile magnificent planet, who eats
and thinks and feels and will someday die: an animal, made of meat.